Select Sermons

Welcoming Grace
Words of Love for All

All sermons in this book were written and delivered by Pastor Kurt Jacobson at Trinity Lutheran Church in Eau Claire, Wisconsin.

Published by eBookIt.com

ISBN-13: 978-1-4566-2642-6

TABLE OF CONTENTS

FOREWORD

By Andra Palmer

This collection of selected sermons by Pastor Kurt Jacobson is a treasure that spans twenty-eight years of service. What an uplifting experience, to go back and revisit Pastor Kurt's most powerful and compelling sermons that bring hope and good news to our lives!

For those of you who were in the congregation when Pastor Kurt delivered these sermons, you will hear his voice and see his body language as you read each one. Your readings will take you back to that year, that church service, that Bible passage, and Kurt's moving message.

If you weren't present for a specific sermon, this compilation will be a guiding post of hope to carry your faith through good times and challenging times. In fact, I encourage you to read these sermons aloud to experience their powerful delivery.

The congregation and guests of Trinity Lutheran Church were blessed to have Pastor Kurt's unique mix of passion, intellect and storytelling from the altar. And he spoke from the first step of the Altar, not from behind a distant pulpit, intimately addressing everyone in the sanctuary.

Pastor Kurt's sermons highlight current events and the daily lives of his congregants, while incorporating rich imagery and stories from the Bible.

For example, I was present in church in April 2011, when Pastor Kurt delivered his Palm Sunday sermon entitled "Two Parades Then, Two Parades

Now." Pastor Kurt presented a viewpoint of Pilate's parade entering Jerusalem from the west and Jesus' parade entering Jerusalem from the "opposite side of town." What a riveting comparison! The description of the pageantry of Pilate's parade, juxtaposed against Jesus' humble parade, and Pastor's relation to current events, provided a thought- provoking and deeply moving experience. Again, Pastor Kurt delivered a powerful message to all.

Now, we can all appreciate and reminisce as we read the collection of Pastor Kurt's selected sermons from his twenty-eight-year career at Trinity Lutheran Church in Eau Claire. Thank you for this generous gift of hope and good news, Pastor Kurt!

***

CONFESSION OF A BLACK SHEEP LUTHERAN UPON THE OCCASION OF A BELOVED PASTOR RETIRING

By Nickolas Butler

I suppose that I have been a member of Trinity Lutheran Church since about the age of eight, when my family moved to 309 East Grant Avenue, less than a mile from Trinity's charismatic ski-sloped roof. In the subsequent twenty-eight years, I cannot brag of perfect attendance, passionate volunteerism, or faithful tithing. I have never once come forward to collect offerings, or sing in the choir.

The truth is I am a very flawed Lutheran. I attend church each Sunday to sit with my wife's family, and to be close to my children. I come to church because I am reminded of my own childhood, sitting beside my father and mother, or poking at my younger brother with a stubby pew-pencil. Or paging through *The Bible* in search of especially violent or prophetic passages (I still turn to "Revelation" on Sunday mornings for a taste of what awaits us down the line: pale horses, avenging angels, a lake of fire – terrible stuff!) I have always enjoyed staring at Trinity's ever-rotating collection of tapestries (they used to be much more prominently displayed back then – my favorite was the lamb and the chalice), or listening to the light drone of traffic off Clairemont.

But I do love listening to a great sermon. Sermons are why I go to church, why I will always attend Trinity. We are all inundated with entertainment in our lives: movies, TV, radio, social media... But sermons are a fantastic reprieve from all that. A time to sit and listen and reflect in ways both intellectual and spiritual. Sermons are a challenge, a charge – a plea to change our mentalities for the better, our world for the better. And for the last twenty-eight years or so, I have been sincerely blessed to spend many Sunday mornings listening to Pastor Kurt Jacobson preach.

It must be very difficult, this preaching business, delivering a compelling sermon. We've all endured lackluster sermons. There are so many ways a sermon can go dreadfully wrong: too erudite, too long, too repetitious, too vague, too pop-culture, too balky, too much money-talk, too much fire and brimstone... A sermon can fail before it ever begins if the pastor has a poor understanding of the guiding scripture, or no clear message that even dovetails the scripture, let allow elucidating it.

As parishioners, we suffer through this all too often with Old Testament passages: someone begets somebody who leads an army and wipes out another army and makes a fiery sacrifice to God and then dies. Huh? What can we glean from that, without leaning on hackneyed platitudes or generalities? Then too, a pastor can get far too academic, citing various theologians or articles until the congregation is having dusky flashbacks to some snoozy college course... Delivering a dynamic sermon, week in and week out for *decades* is tough work. And, I can truly say, that Pastor Kurt's sermons have kept me captivated for years and years and years.

This book is a collection of just some of those sermons, and in reading all of them, I am struck by how fortunate Trinity has been to call Kurt our pastor, our leader, in some cases, our friend. In these sermons, we are reminded of Kurt's deep and abiding intellect, his ability to connect everyday life in the 21st century to ancient scripture, and more than anything, to call our attention to the timelessness of the spirit that binds us all, through religious decency, kindness, and grace. We are also reminded of his adventurousness and daring. Kurt is a world-traveler, and in these sermons, we see him white-water rafting in Alaska or volunteering in a hospital in Haiti.

I don't think it is a coincidence that Trinity's growth in parishioners and the expansion of its worship area happen to correspond with Kurt's tenure at the church. As you can read in his sermons, he very much *invested* his own spirit, in not only the congregation as a body, but also the very building. These sermons illuminate just how passionately he cared for his flock, even for black sheep like me, playing tic-tac-toe or hangman on the back of a church bulletin or offering card.

I must admit that it is with a heavy heart that not only will I have been in attendance for some of Kurt's first sermons as a pastor at Trinity, but now, I must face a future without Kurt's voice in the choir, or his indefatigable, almost jolly, pronouncements from behind the pulpit. I don't know if it was *The Bible* or The Byrds, but someone said, "To everything there is a season, and a time to every purpose under the heaven." Well, now is Kurt's time to retire. To be closer to his aging parents up near Rice Lake. To enjoy his holidays. To travel the world. I don't envy his "successor(s)." I really don't. I can't imagine another pastor, dedicating of themselves more than Kurt has, enriching so many of our Sunday mornings, filling us with so much grace, so much light, so much passion and kindness. What a legacy he has left.

As I have confessed, I may be a bad Lutheran. But I have witnessed a great one. I know what the blueprint looks like, anyway. Thank you, Pastor Kurt, for these wonderful sermons. I wish you all the happiness in the world – you deserve it.

Amen.

***

The Left-Handed Attack

March 4, 1990

Matthew 4:1-11

Then Jesus was led up by the Spirit into the wilderness to be tempted by the devil. He fasted for forty days and forty nights, and afterwards he was famished. The tempter came and said to him, 'If you are the Son of God, command these stones to become loaves of bread.' But he answered, 'It is written, One does not live by bread alone, but by every word that comes from the mouth of God.'

Then the devil took him to the holy city and placed him on the pinnacle of the temple, saying to him, 'If you are the Son of God, throw yourself down; for it is written, 'He will command his angels concerning you,' and 'On their hands they will bear you up, so that you will not dash your foot against a stone.'

Jesus said to him, 'Again it is written, 'Do not put the Lord your God to the test.'

Again, the devil took him to a very high mountain and showed him all the kingdoms of the world and their splendor; and he said to him, 'All these I will give you, if you will fall down and worship me.' Jesus said to him, 'Away with you, Satan! For it is written, 'Worship the Lord your God, and serve only him.'

*Then the devil left him, and suddenly angels came and waited on him.**

Dear Sisters and Brothers,

Grace and peace be yours in abundance through Christ our Lord.

It was the kind of afternoon camp counselors dread. The rain had been falling, heavy and steady, for two days. The dark clouds hovered near the treetops and seemed to promise that the cold, penetrating downpour would continue for yet another day.

Inside the main lodge, an epidemic of cabin fever had broken out. On the first day of rain there were crafts to work on, and a standby ration of wet-weather videos to watch.

The second day of rain passed with group games and a rerun of the videos.

But when the rains continued unabated the third day, the campers were in no mood for videos, crafts, or games. They demanded fresh entertainment. The camp staff was at wits end.

How relieved and pleased the counselors were when a camp visitor, a law enforcement officer, volunteered his services. No he wasn't coming to practice his business. He offered to give the campers a demonstration of weapons, police tactics, and some self-defense procedures.

The assembled campers seemed spellbound to learn how the nightstick and Mace are used. They took turns snapping handcuffs on one another. They listened attentively to the lecture on the dangers of firearms. As a finale, this modern day Elliott Ness showed the campers how best to deal with muggers and stick ups.

Calling a young camper to the platform, he described a fast self-defense action by which one could evade, disarm, and subdue any would-be stickup person who might poke a pistol into your back. The maneuver, he explained, consisted of a quick step to the left, accompanied by a rapid thrust of the right elbow backward and downward to knock away the assailant's revolver. The gun, he promised, would be stripped from the attacker's hand or, at worst, discharge harmlessly into the ground. It all seemed so simple.

With the help of the camper who had now joined him on stage, the lawman proceeded to demonstrate. He armed the camper with a large water pistol. Then assuming the role of the victim, he instructed the camper to approach him from behind and attempt the stickup.

Gun in hand, the would-be robber struck, jabbing the barrel into the victim's back. The bold hero lunged to his left, swung back his right elbow fiercely, and was shot squarely in the back by the junior gunman. The huge, running, water spot between his shoulder blades was clear evidence of the failure of his supposedly safe maneuver.

Red-faced and fumbling for words, the lawman scolded the junior gunman, "You're supposed to hold the gun in your right hand!" But the left-handed robber was not impressed.

Scrambling for some lesson to leave as he beat his retreat, the lawman said, "Well, be sure to watch out for left-handed stickup men."

Every now and then that "lesson" comes back to me, because it is a good one - much like this lesson from Matthew this morning.

The temptation story in the Gospel today tells us how the devil tempted Jesus. The devil here wasn't only left handed - he was ambidextrous! He went straight for the jugular. He called Jesus' authority and position into question. He tried to twist Jesus up with God's own words.

From the time Jesus stepped out of the baptismal river waters to the time he hung from the cross, temptation was near at hand. Over and over it came. It hounded and pursued him at every turn.

It came through mouths of friends and enemies, disciples and demons, kings and plain folk.

From wherever the temptation came, its attack was always certain - it always carried the same theme - God's word of promise was being called into question. The temptations hurled at Jesus were always attempting to call into question who he was, who he belonged to, and who loved him.

The temptation called God's word of promise a lie, something that could not be trusted, something that needed to be tested and verified.

In this Bible account of the devil tempting Jesus, all the angles the devil attempted came down to a simple question, “Would Jesus trust in God's word alone, or would he demand something more?”

Would Jesus hold on to the promise in spite of the devil's cunning arguments, or would he put God to the test? Would he fear, love and trust God above all things, or would he hedge his bets and give the devil his due. Would Jesus be a faithful person, or would he give in to unbelief?

The same questions confront each of us, if we're honest. In Baptism, you have been given a word of promise and certainty. The word is that you have been chosen by the grace of God, and made an heir to God's kingdom. Because of this, your sins are forgiven and salvation and eternal life belong to you. God has decided to always love you and provide for you and protect you from danger and harm. Nothing can alter that fact! It is a promise that neither sin nor death nor the devil can destroy!

Nevertheless, it is just that - a word. It is just a word, syllables that roll off the preacher's tongue; a name spoken as water is poured over a baby's head; a little piece of bread and a sip of wine. The promise of life and salvation is given to you as a word, without proof, without evidence, without objective means of verification today.

It is a word for faith, not sight. It is a word that will either grip you with certainty that it doesn't need to be proved or verified, or it's a word which will be trampled and crushed by your hankering after the logical and provable.

The question is at your doorstep today as it was for Jesus in the wilderness. Will you trust in God's word alone, or will you demand something more? Will you put God to the test?

Will you demand some proof of God before you believe the words of promise?

That is the temptation, and it will hound you and pursue you like it did Jesus. It will assume many voices and variations. I hear them often. The temptations usually arise in questions - honest ones though they be:

"Pastor Kurt, I just don't think that God can love all people. Can God?"

I hear the temptations in the assertions that the word of promise which is forgiveness and grace can't be for those people who never come to church. Or for those minorities or those homosexuals or those liberals or those who don't believe or act the way we do.

I hear the temptations in the statements that God's promise of forgiveness and grace given at Baptism can't do it all - that there has to be something we have to do to finally win the prize.

Perhaps the temptations come in the voice of the cynic: "Yes, you Christians talk about God's love and how God will provide. That will do you a lot of good in the unemployment line! If God cares for you so much, then let God get you a job!"

Or "How can you believe in a God of love, Christian, when your loved one dies a slow, painful death? Is your God so weak or cruel that God could not have done something about it? Is God's promise anything but an empty word?"

Make no mistake. God is a loving God. God does keep promises. It is temptation's voice which challenges this.

We all fall into temptation. The church is no more immune to the temptations than you or I. The church has, too often, been tempted to appease people, to coddle their childish beliefs rather than urge them to rethink their understandings of what it means to be a chosen people. The church falls into temptation when its leaders fail to prod people, and challenge them to struggle with difficult teachings, or to incorporate the heart of Christian teaching in daily living.

The message that God loves all people, that God sees all people as equal, is a tough thing for us to swallow. It's nice to talk about our intentions to love all people. It's nice to think we are inclusive or accepting of people who are different from us.

But it's a wholly different thing to put those concepts into life. Perhaps its temptation's influence when the church is rebuffed in its efforts to be faithful or when the church is pushed into a neat little compartment - a part of our life that only comes into play once a week.

Too often, the church has been reluctant to move from nostalgia, and the ways of the past, in order to make the gospel more palatable and comforting. The truth is, Scripture calls us to rely totally on God's word and scatters us throughout society for the good of our neighbors. The church must always be faithful to the word of God. To settle for anything less is to play into the devil's hand.

Is there a practical meaning for us in this lesson today? This temptation story should strengthen the church and its people. Here we learn that Jesus wouldn't bow to the temptation, instead he relied completely on God. He didn't bemoan the fact, "Why is God doing this to me?" He didn't try to fight it on his own. The good news is that the devil failed with Jesus.

Despite the left-handed attacks, the devil was unable to pry Jesus loose from his trust in God's word. He tried again and again, but Jesus hung on. He hung on at the cross as the temptation came to its climax, "If you are the Son of God, come down from the cross." Jesus held on to the promise.

God freed Jesus. God raised him from the dead. God will free us once and for all, too.

Jesus, the Son of God, is our Lord. That is the best news you could ever hear because it means that the victory he won over unbelief against the devil, he won for you. When you are tempted, torn between faith and unbelief; when the cynics rise up and declare that the promise of your baptism is not enough; when you are confronted with personal crisis - be assured. Be assured that you are following a God who was there before you.

Rejoice and be glad. God will keep you. God has promised to do that. By God's word alone.

Amen.

***

The End of Religion

March 28, 1993

Lent 5A

John 11:1-45 NRSV

Now a certain man was ill, Lazarus of Bethany, the village of Mary and her sister Martha. Mary was the one who anointed the Lord with perfume and wiped his feet with her hair; her brother Lazarus was ill. So the sisters sent a message to Jesus, "Lord, he whom you love is ill." But when Jesus heard it, he said, "This illness does not lead to death; rather it is for God's glory, so that the Son of God may be glorified through it."

Accordingly, though Jesus loved Martha and her sister and Lazarus, after having heard that Lazarus was ill, he stayed two days longer in the place where he was. Then after this he said to the disciples, "Let us go to Judea again." The disciples said to him, "Rabbi, the Jews were just now trying to stone you, and are you going there again?" Jesus answered, "Are there not twelve hours of daylight? Those who walk during the day do not stumble, because they see the light of this world. But those who walk at night stumble, because the light is not in them." After saying this, he told them, "Our friend Lazarus has fallen asleep, but I am going there to awaken him." The disciples said to him, "Lord, if he has fallen asleep, he will be all right."

Jesus, however, had been speaking about his death, but they thought that he was referring merely to sleep. Then Jesus told them plainly, "Lazarus is dead. For your sake I am glad I was not there, so that you may believe. But let us go to him." Thomas, who was called the Twin, said to his fellow disciples, "Let us also go, that we may die with him."

When Jesus arrived, he found that Lazarus had already been in the tomb four days. Now Bethany was near Jerusalem, some two miles away, and many of the Jews had come to Martha and Mary to console them about their brother. When Martha heard that Jesus was coming, she went and met him, while Mary stayed at home. Martha said to Jesus, "Lord, if you had been here, my brother would not have died. But even now I know that God will give you whatever you ask of him." Jesus said to her, "Your brother will rise again." Martha said to him, "I know that he will rise again in the resurrection on the last day."

Jesus said to her, "I am the resurrection and the life. Those who believe in me, even though they die, will live, and everyone who lives and believes in me will never die. Do you believe this?" She said to him, "Yes, Lord, I believe that you are the Messiah, the Son of God, the one coming into the world." When she had said this, she went back and called her sister Mary, and told her privately, "The Teacher is here and is calling for you." And when she heard it, she got up quickly and went to him.

Now Jesus had not yet come to the village, but was still at the place where Martha had met him. The Jews who were with her in the house, consoling her, saw Mary get up quickly and go out. They followed her because they thought that she was going to the tomb to weep there. When Mary came where Jesus was and saw him, she knelt at his feet and said to him, "Lord, if you had been here, my brother would not have died."

When Jesus saw her weeping, and the Jews who came with her also weeping, he was greatly disturbed in spirit and deeply moved. He said, "Where have you laid him?" They said to him, "Lord, come and see." Jesus began to weep. So the Jews said, "See how he loved him!" But some of them said, "Could not he who opened the eyes of the blind man have kept this man from dying?" Then Jesus, again greatly disturbed, came to the tomb.

It was a cave, and a stone was lying against it. Jesus said, "Take away the stone." Martha, the sister of the dead man, said to him, "Lord, already there is a stench because he has been dead four days." Jesus said to her, "Did I not tell you that if you believed, you would see the glory of God?" So they took away the stone. And Jesus looked upward and said, "Father, I thank you for having heard me. I knew that you always hear me, but I have said this for the sake of the crowd standing here, so that they may believe that you sent me." When he had said this, he cried with a loud voice, "Lazarus, come out!" The dead man came out, his hands and feet bound with strips of cloth, and his face wrapped in a cloth. Jesus said to them, "Unbind him, and let him go."

Many of the Jews therefore, who had come with Mary and had seen what Jesus did, believed in him.

Dear Friends,

Grace and peace to you from God and our Lord and Savior, Jesus Christ.

Have you noticed how much there's been in the news on the subject of religion lately?

In the past three weeks, the covers of *Newsweek, Time* and *U.S. News and World Report* magazines have had religious themes. If you didn't see any of those magazines, you can probably guess that the press religion has been getting isn't good.

Religion has been taking it on the chin these past few weeks with the Branch Davidian ordeal in Texas, the Muslims being accused of bombing the World Trade Center, and anti-abortion Christians turning violent in Florida. Throughout time, religion has been controversial.

Clark Morphew, a Lutheran pastor, writes a column in the *St. Paul Pioneer Press,* and yesterday, wrote about a young man telling of a religion class he's taking at a Twin Cities Christian university.

The teacher of the class gave the students an assignment. The students were to give one-word descriptions of religion. Maybe we should do that here? Of the 15 students' answers, none were positive. All were negative words and most were associated with conflict.

Maybe the truth is that religion is full of conflict. Negative things do happen, even in the most religious gatherings of people. When you look at the past decade of religious history, there has been a load of conflict, and none of it was pretty.

Just about anywhere you look, all around the world, religions are in conflict, and experts are saying it may continue forever. These ethnic and religious hatreds run deeper than faith, and they will spill over every time society allows one group to publicly hate another.

Why is there so often, no tolerance, much less love between religious people? Why, if religion is our expression of belief in God, is it so often times cruel, vicious and divisive?

There's a story that comedian Emo Philips tells about two Baptists. I'm not singling out Baptists - we could substitute Lutherans for Baptists in the story. Before I tell you the story, there is one word you need to know to get a chuckle - and it's the word "heretic."

To be called a heretic is not a compliment! A "heretic" is a person who holds an opinion or belief about religion that deviates from the norm or the standard. Emo Philips, this comedian, talks about a time when he met someone new and right away discovered that their religious backgrounds were very much alike.

I said, “Are you Protestant or Catholic?"

He said, "Protestant."

I said, "Me too! What franchise?"

He said, "Baptist."

I said, "Me too!"

He said, "Northern Baptist."

I said, "Me too!"

The two men go back and forth like this for a while. Then Philips asks, "Are you Northern conservative fundamentalist Baptist - Great Lakes Region Council of 1879, or Northern Great Lakes Region Council of 1912?"

The other fellow says, 'Northern conservative fundamentalist Baptist - Great Lakes Region Council of 1912."

Philip replies, "Die heretic!"

Philip's story is not too far off the mark, nor is it limited to Baptists. We all know, some of us from firsthand experience, religion very often divides people and closes them off from one another.

Lutherans and Roman Catholics fostered mistrust for each other for years.

Today, some still hold <u>their</u> religion to be THEE most holy and proper. But I ask you, "Why does religion have these negative effects? Why does it divide people?"

I think I'd like to venture an answer to that question. The problem with religion is thinking that we have all the answers - and that our way is the right way.

The rub comes when someone else believes there is another way - another means of ascribing glory to God - and we cannot tolerate that other way.

We think our way is most excellent, and we will not explore new avenues or consider different thinking. When we refuse to be open to new ideas and new learning, and begin to channel our energies into preserving the status quo, then religion becomes a curse.

This was the situation of the Pharisees we read about today who were put out by Jesus and his work of bringing Lazarus back from the dead. These Pharisees were good and proper religious people. They had in their heritage all the richness and vibrancy of Jewish religious experience. They wanted to preserve that tradition, even as it had become cramping and deadly.

Many times in the Gospels, we read about the tension religious people felt toward Jesus. I think the religious people of that day would have been happier if Jesus had never appeared on the scene.

I can almost hear the Pharisees saying, "What are we to you, Jesus? Mind your own business, Jesus. Just leave and let us get back to our old-time religion. We don't need you or your new ways of doing things!"

Are people still saying that today? You bet. Religion can get in the way of our believing and following Jesus Christ. Religion has said that people who didn't conform to all our beliefs aren't welcome. Religion has said that people who don't believe in the prescribed ways are wrong or bad. Old-time religion has said that sexuality is bad, and so are working mothers and the divorced.

Old-time religion has said that Christianity is really about not drinking, not smoking, not dancing, not playing cards. For women, old-time religion has meant wearing only a certain amount of makeup and sensible shoes.

For men, it meant having the proper haircut, and joining the civic club, and putting bread on the table. And for the people who didn't fit this view of Christianity, old-time religion was all too eager and all too quick to say, "Die, heretic."

The religious establishment, as portrayed in the Bible, would have loved it. That's the thing about old-time religion - it always tends to be the same. Religion that hates change will certainly try to stop anything new. That kind of religion is not good. It’s not good enough for me, or for you, or for anyone. That kind of religion is cramping and deadly and it needs to end.

So, do we want new-time religion? No. Jesus did not come to bring a new religion to this earth. Jesus put an end to religion as the Bible makes clear.

You see the problem - the whole point with <u>religion</u> is that you have to do something. With religion, you have to offer sacrifices or offerings, or you have to eat fish on Fridays, or you have to abstain from dancing or drinking or you have to wear your best to church and on and on.

All religions are about doing something so that God will change his mind about us.

The problem with all religions is that they assume that God really doesn't like us very much. Religions assume that God is full of demands and anger, and needs to be bought off or pacified.

Jesus' teaching, on the other hand, is radically different. Jesus said that God didn't need to be bought off. Jesus said that God is a God of mercy and acceptance, new hope and fresh starts. No wonder the religious establishment reacted so strongly to Jesus. Jesus proclaimed the end of religion and a new way of living as believing, faithful people.

A student of the great theologian Karl Barth once asked him if God had revealed himself in any other religion besides Christianity. Barth said, "No, God has not revealed himself in any religion, including Christianity. God has revealed himself in his Son!"

That, my friends, is most important! We do not gather as the faith community of Trinity on Sunday morning as members of the Christian religion; we gather as the community of Jesus Christ to share new life in the Savior.

Let me say that again because the first part of that sentence may have been too shocking to hear the whole thing: We do not gather as the faith community of Trinity on Sunday morning as members of the Christian religion; we gather as the community of Jesus Christ to share new life in the Savior.

That means that we gather to celebrate salvation, not religion.

The word "religion" comes from a Latin word that means, "To bind together." The word "salvation" comes from a word that means "to become large." Even the derivations of the words suggest that "religion" can mean something bound up and cramped, while "salvation" means something spacious, having room, being opened up.

The community of Jesus is about salvation. It is not cramped, but expansive; not closed, but open; not something bound up, but something that gives us room.

The community of Jesus Christ lives out of forgiveness, not guilt; affirmation rather than shame. Religion has heaped enough guilt on people to last until the end of time.

The community of Jesus Christ is characterized not by laws and rules, but my music and songs; not by policies and doctrine, but by love and hope and faith. The community of Jesus is open to all.

The community of Jesus Christ is not about religion, but salvation. That should have great impact on your life right now. It should change the way you think - how and why you treat your family, friends, coworkers, students, teachers, pastor with love and kindness, tolerance and respect.

The community of Jesus Christ will continue. As for religion? Well, you can figure that out for yourself.

For now, let's enjoy being this community of Jesus Christ.

Amen.

***

When I Find Myself in Times of Trouble

June 12, 1994

Pentecost 3/B

Genesis 3:8-15

They heard the sound of the Lord God walking in the garden at the time of the evening breeze, and the man and his wife hid themselves from the presence of the Lord God among the trees of the garden. But the Lord God called to the man, and said to him, 'Where are you?'

The man said, 'I heard the sound of you in the garden, and I was afraid, because I was naked; and I hid myself.'

God said, 'Who told you that you were naked? Have you eaten from the tree of which I commanded you not to eat?'

The man said, 'The woman whom you gave to be with me, she gave me fruit from the tree, and I ate.'

Then the Lord God said to the woman, 'What is this that you have done?'

The woman said, 'The serpent tricked me, and I ate.'

The Lord God said to the serpent, 'Because you have done this, cursed are you among all animals and among all wild creatures; upon your belly you shall go, and dust you shall eat all the days of your life.'

I will put enmity between you and the woman, and between your offspring and hers; he will strike your head, and you will strike his heel.

Dear Friends,

Grace and peace to you.

Back in December of 1987, during my last year at Luther Seminary I enrolled in a short course on rural ministry. I had heard that 54% of Lutheran churches were in rural areas, and 77% of first-time pastors went to those rural churches. So, I figured this course just might help me have some idea of the challenges that could await.

It was a great course. We spent time at the Minneapolis Grain Exchange and the State Agriculture Department. We visited with officials from the Farm Credit Bureau and CENEX.

One week of this course included a field experience: being assigned to work with a pastor in a rural setting, and living on a farm. I was assigned to Elbow Lake, Minnesota and Pastor Paul Pederson. Paul did a great job of immersing me in the culture and color of rural life.

We spent time each morning in the local cafes, visiting with everyone who came through the door. I attended church meetings in the evenings which were always followed by “lunch” which consisted of sandwiches, green jello, homemade pickles, donuts and coffee.

There were two days in this rural ministry class that are still prominent in my memory, all these years later. One was the privilege of spending a day with the local veterinarian, Bob Hagen.

Having grown up with a dog and spent a few days each summer on a friend's farm, I did have some clue as to what a vet did, but I had never experienced any of it firsthand.

It wasn't long after Jim dropped me off at the clinic that we were in Bob’s pickup truck, heading to the Lindloff farm. They were one of only a few dairy farmers in this grain farming county.

It was time for a regular vaccination of the Lindloff's dairy herd and a "pregnancy" check of the cows. Coming out of the seminary in St. Paul, I had forgotten my coveralls and rubber boots, but Dr. Bob was kind enough to outfit me before I accompanied him into the barnyard. It was a bright, mild December day, warm enough so nothing was frozen. Bob introduced me to Farmer Lindloff and we were off to work.

The cows were ushered out of the barn and into a stanchion, where they would be secured for the vaccination and "pregnancy" test. My job was to operate the gate to release the cow after all necessary tasks had been performed.

You might imagine the determined haste with which the cow departed the stanchion after having the pregnancy test performed by the arm of a good sized man. Suffice it to say the coveralls were helpful - and a large hat with wide brim would have been appreciated.

Then there was the second memorable day of this class. During the week, I had the privilege of living on two different farms. My first host was James Carlson, a bachelor, who, as an only child had taken care of his parents until they died and now continued on the family farm.

With a penchant for electronics, post-it notes and toothpicks, his house was like nothing I had ever seen. James knew the back roads of the entire county, and every time we went somewhere he took me down another road.

That Sunday, I was to visit both churches that Pastor Paul served - the Norwegian one in the country and the Swedish one in Elbow Lake metro.

The Norwegians had their service first - at 9am. James was Swedish and went to the church in town. So he sent me off with hurried directions to the Norwegian church in the country. Now remember, he knew the country roads like the palm of his hand. I on the other hand, who had been confused every time we got in the car, managed to get completely lost.

Driving around with great haste, frantically trying to get my bearings and with a hollow feeling in my stomach, I never made it to the little Norwegian church where I was to assist with the worship service. By about 9:30 I managed to find my way to the Swedish church in town where I hid from everyone, waiting with great embarrassment for Pastor Paul to show up. Luckily, when Paul did arrive, he had humorously played up my absence with the Norwegians and was looking forward to letting the Swedes in on my trouble.

In trouble. Depending on who you are, being "in trouble" can mean a variety of things.

*If you're a kid, it can be the result of disobeying mom or dad.

*For a teenager, it can happen from staying out too late.

*If you're a teacher, it can mean having to deal with uncooperative students.

*If you're the accountant in your home, trouble can mean a shortfall in the checkbook at bill-paying time.

*For farmers, trouble comes in the form of breakdowns, infestations, frost, and drought.

I think it's safe to say, that no matter **who** we are - no matter what **age** we are - or what **occupation** we're in - or **where** we live, we **all** have times in our lives when we get in trouble. Times when our lives become disrupted. When we're faced with a crisis, or some kind of stress. Times when we have to adjust our lives. When we have to change and adapt to some new element that's been thrust, often unwillingly, into our lives.

*For the child or teenager, it often means accepting the discipline of parents.

*For the family bill-payer, it can mean sitting down with creditors to square away one's finances.

*For the farmer it may mean having to use sprays, losing a crop, or worse.

Regardless, trouble **disrupts**. Trouble **interrupts**. Trouble challenges us to rethink and change.

And the common denominator of all trouble, is that not one of us is immune to it. All of us, sooner or later get into it. At some point in our lives, most of us daily, and I include myself in that group, have to deal with trouble. It's a fact of life. Things fail. Relationships break up. We break down.

The Bible reading from Genesis, the third chapter, offers us some guidance in dealing with trouble. Specifically, Genesis shows us how **God responds when we get in trouble.**

This bible story from Genesis has gotten into its own trouble from time to time. Attempts to use these verses to understand the origin of evil, or to place blame on God, or each other, for the origins of sin have been unhelpful.

Some of you have heard sermons on these verses or received instruction that stresses the shame of the first humans, and therefore the shame of all of us before God.

Other people look to this Bible story and want to focus on the serpent's curse and ask questions which are impossible to answer. Just the other night, I watched a television preacher equating Adam's hiding from God in the Garden to the way the alcoholic hides behind the bottle.

Suffice it to say that the greater learning in this story is **how God responds when we get in trouble.**

This is precisely the claim of Scripture today: That God - the One who created us, knows us and watches over us responds in times of trouble and uncertainty.

In Genesis 3, Adam and Eve have just eaten from the tree of the forbidden fruit - eaten what they weren't supposed to.

God had given very specific instructions to leave that tree alone, and if they did eat from it, they would immediately die. So after eating, they withdrew and hid in the trees. They knew they did wrong. They feared big trouble was headed their way. So they hid.

God, in the meantime the Bible tells us, is out in the garden taking a walk and enjoying the trees in the evening breeze. God created the trees specifically to enjoy their beauty, we learn in a previous verse. I like to picture God enjoying this evening stroll and to make the evening even more pleasant, God looks for that man and woman who had been created to enjoy the garden too. But on this evening, the pair isn't out enjoying the creation. They've gotten into to trouble, big time, and now they're hiding from God who told them not to eat of that tree.

God calls out to Adam, "Where are you?" That's it, "Where are you?"

Of course, God knew where they were. Of course, God knew exactly what tree they were hiding behind. God had created these two humans with God's own hands. They were God's children. It bothered God that Adam and Eve had been disobedient, and so God went looking for them.

Now, I don't know about you, but whenever I was in trouble as a kid, my mother never just said, "Where are you?"

But with Adam and Eve, God simply calls, "Where are you?"

There's no threat, no demands, no anger expressed. Nothing more forthcoming but the simple question, "Where are you?"

God doesn't step into Adam's trouble and berate, accuse or sentence. But God also doesn't come in with some big miracle and instantaneously right a wrong situation, either.

All God did was to help them know where they were. God said, "Where are you? Stop for a minute and look at where you are, Adam, and what has just happened."

God gently gave them a place to start, in their going from a position of trouble and helplessness, to one of wholeness.

What marvelous examples today for us, this Adam and Eve - for those times when we get in trouble. During those times when we get confused and mixed up. When we withdraw into hiding like Adam. Times when we don't know what to do. During those times when we are at a loss to figure out what the problem is that got us into such dire straits.

Remember God's words to Adam, "Where are you?"

We are God's children. God made each one of us. God cares when we get ourselves into messes. Like a good and loving parent, God wants to help us in such a way so we can figure out how we got into trouble. God wants to help us in such a way that we don't make the same mistake again and again. That's how God helps us.

Finally, what is the outcome of God's assistance? It's getting on with business. Simply that. In the case of Adam and Eve, nothing miraculous came of God's help. God provided them clothes so they wouldn't have to be embarrassed in their nakedness. God enabled them to get back to the business of living.

Of course, they had to move to another neighborhood. God helped them even in that, and they continued on. In the same way God wants to help us, only insomuch as it will help us to get on with our lives.

God knows we have families, duties, jobs and dreams. God knows we don't like to spend our entire life wallowing in a state of confusion or despair or trouble.

That's why when God sees us in trouble, God says, "Where are you, Kurt?" "Where are you, Chris, Tom, Nancy?" "Where are you <u>my</u> child?"

Friends, God knows we get in trouble. It's part of life. But even better, God wants to help us see our way out of our trouble.

Remember that. And may God give to each of us, the spirit of wisdom and understanding, to see us through our difficulties and towards peace and wholeness with God and each other.

Amen.

***

Drawing Lines

October 15, 1995

Pentecost 19/C

Luke 16:19-31

There was a rich man who was dressed in purple and fine linen and who feasted sumptuously every day. And at his gate lay a poor man named Lazarus, covered with sores, who longed to satisfy his hunger with what fell from the rich man's table; even the dogs would come and lick his sores.

The poor man died and was carried away by the angels to be with Abraham. The rich man also died and was buried. In Hades, where he was being tormented, he looked up and saw Abraham far away with Lazarus by his side. He called out, "Father Abraham, have mercy on me, and send Lazarus to dip the tip of his finger in water and cool my tongue; for I am in agony in these flames."

But Abraham said, "Child, remember that during your lifetime you received your good things, and Lazarus in like manner evil things; but now he is comforted here, and you are in agony. Besides all this, between you and us a great chasm has been fixed, so that those who might want to pass from here to you cannot do so, and no one can cross from there to us."

He said, "Then, father, I beg you to send him to my father's house— for I have five brothers—that he may warn them, so that they will not also come into this place of torment."

Abraham replied, "They have Moses and the prophets; they should listen to them."

He said, "No, father Abraham; but if someone goes to them from the dead, they will repent."

He said to him, "If they do not listen to Moses and the prophets, neither will they be convinced even if someone rises from the dead."

Dear Sisters and Brothers;

Grace and peace be with you all.

The story is told of a hitchhiker picked up one day out on the road. As he got into the car, the driver squealed the tires, pulling back into traffic. The hitchhiker was startled but didn't say anything. A little way down the road, the hitchhiker glanced over at the speedometer and was shocked. Breaking his silence, he exclaimed, "Wow, you're going 67 in a 35 mph zone."

The driver responded casually, "Don't worry, God is with us."

They continued zipping through an intersection, not slowing a bit.

"Hey! You just ran that stop sign!"

The reply, "Don't worry; God is with us."

Finally, after taking a corner on two wheels, the hitchhiker shouted, "Stop the car!"

"Why? Didn't I tell you? God is with us."

"Yeah, I know," the hitchhiker shot back. "Stop the car anyway, "God and I want to get out!"

Have you ever spent much time trying to figure out what makes people tick? What motivates certain behaviors?

Throughout human history, scientists have been trying to figure us out. Some have come up with theories. You've heard of them.

Eugene Skinner believed our behavior was motivated by the desire to experience pleasure over pain. Sigmund Freud believed that sex was the driving force behind all we do. Economists believe that it is money, and our desire to have it, that lies at the root of all human activity.

There is one branch of human thought among some behavioral psychologists that suggests all our actions and all our motivations grow out of one desire - the need to establish and protect our own territory.

Now think about that - we all have our territories. I recall in college studying about the space bubble - that invisible bubble around our bodies that defines for us the distance we keep when in contact with another person.

Americans have a much larger space bubble than some Europeans. Americans like about a three-foot space bubble. When someone we do not know, or do not share a close or intimate relationship with, gets inside that space bubble, we pull back or withdraw.

The experts in this idea of territory theory, go so far as to say this is the reason birds sing, insects buzz and swarm, and dogs bark and bite. In humans, the territorial theory can explain everything from why some people seem to spend all their "free time" taking care of their yard, to the on-going nature of ethnic wars.

Because we are territorial people, we draw lines. Mostly, we like to draw lines around things, people and property, and declare everything inside that line as "mine" or "ours." Remember drawing the lines on the back seat of the station wagon, showing your brother or sister where that line was, just exactly what space was yours, and warning them of the dangers of crossing that line?

Robert Frost, in one of his poems, stated that, "good fences make good neighbors." Makes me think of Sun City, Arizona, and some other places that I've been in which every yard is entombed by a ten-foot-high concrete wall. The message I get when I see this is, "Stay away, this is my property - do not enter without permission."

In our own countryside, "No Trespass" signs warn us not to step over the line.

We're very good at drawing lines to keep our territories. The lines we draw around what is "ours," and what is others', varies from situation to situation.

- When people trespass against us by touching a "soft spot" where we are vulnerable to offense, even if the intrusion is accidental or ignorant or a poor attempt at humor, we begin to defend "our space."
- When the neighbor's dog does something inside the boundary of our lawn, we know exactly where the point of trespass lies, "our yard."
- When a wave of robberies begins to haunt our side of town, our territorial line suddenly expands to include "our neighborhood."
- When we resent the intrusion by the federal government into our regional needs or wants, our territory takes on the even larger boundaries of "our state."
- When federal spending is out of control, and costs of governmental assistance to immigrants increase, we suddenly want to keep foreign people out and protect "our nation."
- When the ozone layer starts to fizzle away from CFC's, and our oceans start smelling like

backed-up septic tanks, we suddenly feel the need to defend "our planet."

Do you see how it is that we draw lines so broadly and wide that they encompass the whole earth? When threatened or denied security or desires, we draw lines to protect ourselves.

But notice how the line gets so broad and wide that it becomes a circle. From drawing lines around our homes, neighborhood, state, nation and planet, we've drawn a circle! Every living creature is "inside" the circle, the boundary we've drawn!

This is the kind of line, an eternal, never-ending line resulting in a circle, that Jesus wanted to call attention to in the Bible story you heard a few minutes ago. The rich man, during his life on earth, had drawn lines very tightly around himself and his possessions. The poor man, named Lazarus, lived in misery and hunger just outside the lines of the rich man.

When the rich man died, he reached a new territory. The Bible calls it "Hades," and suddenly this man who had lived the good life was now on the wrong side of the line.

The poor man, on the other hand, died and was carried away by angels to be with Abraham and enjoy the good life on the right side of the line that he had not experienced on earth. It was a complete reversal of fortune for each man.

The rich man, only after he found himself on the wrong side of the line, realized his error while on earth. He finally realized that he should have reached out to the poor man when he had time. But he did not do so, and by his failure to act, built a huge gap, a big fat line between himself and the poor man.

As the rich man discovers his error, he begs Father Abraham to enact a rescue operation and send the poor man to bring him some relief!

Imagine his gall, we might think. This rich guy didn't care a speck about the poor man when he was suffering, and now this rich guy wants some mercy and relief?

Father Abraham declares that it's too late for the rich man. In so many words, Abraham tells the rich man, "You drew the line long ago and you refused to broaden your line, to open up your territory to help the poor right around you. The gap you created is too large to be crossed."

The rich man isn't completely dissuaded yet. So he tries again, this time for the benefit of his five brothers still on earth.

"Father Abraham, if the gap is so large that I cannot be saved, then at least send the poor man back from the dead so that he can warn my five brothers, that they be spared my fate." Again, the answer is "no."

Abraham says, "They have been taught what the Bible has to say and they should listen. But if they do not listen, then they surely won't be convinced if someone comes back from the dead."

End of story.

In my mind, I try to imagine what came next. I want the story to continue. I want to hear the rest of the dialogue. Did the brothers ever get the message and broaden their lines? We aren't told. For that is the question the story leaves for us to answer. And to answer the question, we need to look at the lines we've drawn in our lives.

Think about it for a moment. What lines have you drawn? Are you so busy protecting yourself that you fail to see and act for the poor at your doorstep?

Is your life increasingly subdivided by lines? What lines keep you from interacting with the Hmong in our community or the poor, or the homeless? And I wonder what we are teaching our children about lines?

Where are we drawing the lines as we teach children to have compassion for and act on behalf of people in need?

Even in the church, there are lines and we all draw them. There are lines between old and young, married and single, long-time members and newer, those with wealth and those with modest means.

This congregation is about to cross a big, fat line next Sunday. One week from tonight for the first time, we'll be welcoming homeless families into our building for a week-long stay.

As a host congregation in the new Interfaith Hospitality Network, we'll be housing homeless families for five one-week stays a year. This new ministry will cross lines for many of us.

We have a stigma attached to the homeless. We consider homeless people to be lazy or poor decision makers, drug-users, alcoholics. If this is your opinion, I urge you especially, to get involved by being a part of Trinity's hospitality to homeless families - and bring your children too.

By our participation in the hospitality network, we're eliminating the lines, bridging the gap. I think that's what Jesus wants us to do. Get rid of the lines, and instead draw a big, expansive circle.

The only way for us to escape from these lines, wherever they may be in our lives, is to draw together all the lines and create the eternal line, the circle.

That circle is made by Jesus Christ. Jesus was always crossing lines, and every time he did so, he upset people to the point of being put to death. But that didn't stop him, because his mission was to eliminate the lines and draw a circle.

Jesus Christ draws a circle around all people. Jesus draws circles of love, circles of hope, circles of peace, and circles of hospitality.

Back to the Bible story for a moment. I don't want you to leave this morning despairing for the rich man. I want you to learn from his mistake.

The rich man in his dire straits was a man loved by God. He was never outside the circle of God's love. However, the rich man just didn't seem to get it. Maybe he was dense or hard-headed. I think he was just plain self-absorbed. He didn't follow God's ways when he had the opportunity. He was so caught up in his own good life.

God did try to teach him how to live. God sent people to teach him. God gave him an abundance of money and possessions with which to be generous. God even sent that poor man to him, so the rich man could practice compassion and generosity. Yet he didn't.

The rich man refused to listen, to see, and most importantly, he failed to act. In spite of it all, God in amazing love sent Jesus to break through those dividing lines, bringing the circle of life.

Today, I hope you'll look at your life and examine the lines you've drawn. Do they form a circle, or are they drawn to keep out others, to protect your money and your possession and your time? In other words, how are you living your life with respect to the needs which exist around us all? Do your lines define a narrow territory or are they expansive and inclusive in the ways that Jesus Christ showed us?

You know the truth of God's teaching - to care for your neighbor, to give your money and time to benefit the less fortunate - to draw a circle of love that encompasses the whole world.

Let's pray:

Gracious God, save us from insensitivity and unconcern for the poor. In our wealth and security, open our eyes to the needs of those who have less. Give us the grace to live for more than our own wants and desires. Enable us to rise above materialism and greed, and decisively act in your ways by giving and sharing and bringing hope to others.

Amen.

***

A Clear Bias

February 15, 1998

Epiphany 6/C

Luke 6:17-26

He came down with them and stood on a level place, with a great crowd of his disciples and a great multitude of people from all Judea, Jerusalem, and the coast of Tyre and Sidon. They had come to hear him and to be healed of their diseases; and those who were troubled with unclean spirits were cured. And all in the crowd were trying to touch him, for power came out from him and healed all of them.

Then he looked up at his disciples and said:
'Blessed are you who are poor,
for yours is the kingdom of God.
'Blessed are you who are hungry now,
for you will be filled.
'Blessed are you who weep now,
for you will laugh.

'Blessed are you when people hate you, and when they exclude you, revile you, and defame you on account of the Son of Man. Rejoice on that day and leap for joy, for surely your reward is great in heaven; for that is what their ancestors did to the prophets.

'But woe to you who are rich,
for you have received your consolation.
'Woe to you who are full now,
for you will be hungry.

'Woe to you who are laughing now,
for you will mourn and weep.
'Woe to you when all speak well of you, for that is what their ancestors did to the false prophets.

Dear Sisters and Brothers;

May the grace and peace of God in Christ be yours in abundance this day, and always. Amen.

In a Peanuts comic strip one day, Lucy reports to Charlie Brown saying, "I have examined my life and have found it to be without flaw! Therefore, I'm going to hold a ceremony and present myself with a medal. I will then give a moving acceptance speech. And after that, I'll greet myself in the receiving line." Lucy concludes, "When you're so good, you just have to do everything yourself."

Have you ever known a Lucy? Someone who is so self-confident, so self-reliant? These folks set extremely high expectations for themselves.

As I have pondered and studied today's Bible reading from Luke in the past week, I've thought about expectations. Sometimes we set so many expectations for ourselves. We want to be the best doctor, lawyer, or teacher. We want to be the good parent, coach, math student, jazz band member, basketball player.

However, I would guess that we're better at setting expectations for other people. I know that in the years that I've been a pastor, I've bumped into many expectations people have for me because of my position. It has happened that people have expected me to know when they're hospitalized, become unemployed, or are having marriage difficulties, so that I might offer pastoral care.

In those situations, where someone has expectations for us, without communicating them to us, hard feelings are sure to be the result.

Whatever the expectations we set for ourselves or others, I have a question that I want you to think about as we gather here today to worship God.

"What are your expectations of God?"

Have you ever thought about that? To me, it's an intriguing question: "What are my expectations of God?" With what agenda do you seek God here today in this gathering?

I've been asking that question of others, and the responses have been interesting.

Joel says, "I expect that God is always going to be there for me."

Megan says, "I expect that God is going to always love me, no matter what."

Ken says, "I expect that God is going to give me eternal life."

Amy says, "I expect that God is going to forgive me, and will help me forgive others and myself."

Earl says, "I expect that God is going to bless me and help me do right in my life."

Now, if I were Oprah, I'd be hopping on down to you and soliciting your responses. In a way, I'd like to do that! To save anyone from embarrassment, I will refrain.

In my interviews on expectations of God, I was not surprised. They were all good responses and probably quite representative of American Christians.

What I didn't hear is an expectation of God that calls forth anything from us. Well, today's Bible reading does just that very clearly. ***"I expect that God is going to change me."***

Would you like to hold such an expectation of God? Did you come here this morning hoping that God's Word would really challenge you?

Well, that's the agenda that God has for us today in the Bible reading from Luke.

Jesus is blatant in setting an expectation for each and every one of us. He expects that we who have money, power, and good lives will work to improve the lives of those who do not have such things.

Jesus knows that our money, our position and our reputation all too easily become a means by which we think we are self-sufficient. People even think that their wealth and status are a blessing from God.

If you doubt me, look again at Jesus' words today. He says:

"Blessed are you who are poor, hungry or excluded - for your reward is great in heaven."

Then he said:

"Woe to you who are rich,

Woe to you who have full stomachs,

Woe to you who laugh now,

For the day is coming when you won't be rich, you will be hungry and you will weep."

Is that challenging enough? I think so! And to be honest, Jesus' words make me nervous, not happy, and a bit ill-at-ease.

Let's face facts: We live in a very, very privileged society! We are rich people. We live in a society that rewards those who make their own way! We are told to set our goals high, to grab for all we can get, to ensure our own future. Accumulate your wealth now so you can be independent in your retirement. It's a "get ahead world," and it's up to you to get yourself ahead!

Then you come here for this time of worship, and you hear the words of Jesus which are totally opposite the ways of the world. Jesus talks about rewarding the poor, the hungry and the sad, and he says the rich, the full, and the happy are not blessed.

Clearly, God has a bias towards the poor; and my friends, we are not the poor. The blessings of God reverse human values we hold dear.

Just looking around at our Midwestern, middle-income lives, I think we could rewrite these words of Jesus and feel better about them. How about this:

"Blessed are the pushers, for they get ahead in the world,

Blessed are the hard-boiled, for they never let life hurt them,

Blessed are those who complain, for they get their own way in the world,

Blessed are the slave-drivers, for they get results,

Blessed are the knowledgeable people of the world, for they know their way around,

Blessed are the trouble-makers, for they make people take notice of them."

This approach to life by some people contradicts the way of life designed by God.

Jesus' words of woe condemn our human values.

I am the first to admit that Jesus words of "woe" hit me. We are not poor people by the world's standard of poor. Yes, we're reluctant to admit we're rich. It's so easy to look at others and see their wealth as so much more than ours. If you've traveled beyond this country, you have seen other standards of living, quite unlike the prominent standard we have in the U.S.

In four weeks, a few dozen people from this congregation will be in Jamaica as part of a congregational mission trip where we'll be working with the poor of that island. For many in our group, this will be their first time to see whole neighborhoods and cities of people living in squalor.

When we leave the Kingston airport, en route to our hotel, we will pass through neighborhoods where corrugated steel and scrap lumber form homes for young families. In that moment, it will be hard, virtually impossible to say, "I'm not a rich person."

Our new missionaries, Tom and Eunice Olson and their three young children, live in the Central African Republic. They recently wrote us a letter as they were preparing to return to Africa after a few months here in America. They wrote:

"The American culture of consumerism is so overwhelming and addictive that it blinds everyone to its toxicity while it snares us in its trap."

To us rich people, Jesus says, WOE!

To us well-fed people, Jesus says, WOE!

To us people who are praised and respected by others, Jesus says, WOE!

Why is Jesus saying these things? Is Jesus a big spoil sport? Doesn't the world go 'round because there are people with money who employ others so that they too can provide for themselves? Isn't a basic aspect of life to be respected and spoken well of?

The "woe" words of Jesus, spelled w-o-e, might be more enlightening for <u>us</u> when spelled w-h-o-a, the word used to stop a horse or someone in the hallway.

Jesus is giving us a stern warning, "Whoa, slow down, stop for a moment to think about your life and your values."

Jesus wants us to remember that we are made to be blessings to other people. Jesus shows us God's bias for the poor, hungry, and sad. So, where does that leave us? How are we to live?

As Christians, well-fed and wealthy by the standard of the world, we must look to Jesus and how he lived. Giving of himself, spurning worldly values and anything, anything at all that, diverted his vision of God's kingdom.

Perhaps we must first stop and ask ourselves, "Do the values I hold fit with God's ways made known in Jesus? Do the decisions I make about how I live, spend my money and share my time reflect God's love and care to the poor and hungry of this world?"

I continue to struggle with Jesus' words - and even my own words today. I have wrestled with them all week.

Finally, I ask myself, "Is there any good news for me and you in these words of Jesus today?"

Surely there is - but to decipher it without first struggling with Jesus' strong teaching about our rich, privileged lives, misses the point. I am condemned by Jesus' teaching. The "woes" are for me and you. I am forced, as disquieting and unpleasant as it may be, to rethink and adjust my life's values.

So where is the good news? The good news is that we have a God who gives us signs in our lives that are intended to redirect our thinking and acting.

I am grateful that God holds expectations for us that call forth from us changes in attitudes and behaviors. It is only through the power of Christ at work in our lives that the present woes of our times can be reversed.

When the words of Jesus today become effective, they redirect our values and actions and change our lives so that we might more clearly reflect the ways of God. That is good news.

Let's pray: Gracious God, we know that it is your desire that we live in your ways each day; so that our lives, our actions, our decisions, our thoughts be in keeping with your bias for the poor. However God, we don't do so well in that. Today, the words of Jesus are tough; they rub and unsettle us because we find that you don't condone our nice, comfortable lives. Continue to stir in us, that in the days ahead, we might be brought to the light of Your ways; and continually re-orient our lives in the same fashion. Through Jesus Christ our Lord.

Amen.

***

But You Promised

March 29, 1998

Lent 5/C

Isaiah 43:16-21

Thus says the Lord,
who makes a way in the sea,
a path in the mighty waters,
who brings out chariot and horse,
army and warrior;
they lie down, they cannot rise,
they are extinguished, quenched like a wick:
Do not remember the former things,
or consider the things of old.
I am about to do a new thing;
now it springs forth, do you not perceive it?
I will make a way in the wilderness
and rivers in the desert.
The wild animals will honor me,
the jackals and the ostriches;
for I give water in the wilderness,
rivers in the desert,
to give drink to my chosen people,
the people whom I formed for myself
so that they might declare my praise.

Dear Sisters and Brothers in Christ,
Grace and peace be with you.

Last Saturday evening, a week ago, a group of three dozen from this congregation returned from an eight-day mission trip to the island of Jamaica. It was a wonderful week.

As one of the leaders, I did not envision such a thoroughly marvelous experience. Our people were fine ambassadors of this congregation and there are many people in Jamaica who now know about Trinity Lutheran Church.

Together with two other congregations who joined our mission trip, we worked at a school in the city of Kingston. We numbered 74 in all, ranging in age from nine to 80. The work that such a large group of people could accomplish in a few days was amazing. There were many aspects to our mission work. We focused on three projects: medical, education and construction.

Our medical team of doctors, nurses and a dentist did health screening on more than 300 first, second and third grade children, most of whom had never seen a health professional before. It was a delight to see our doctors and nurses encountering these children with such care, compassion and friendliness.

The teachers in our group conducted lessons and activities in the classrooms that inspired the children in new ways. It was heartwarming to see American and Jamaican teachers cooperating and the children benefitting.

The rest of us did manual labor like laying a concrete block wall for a new bathroom and improving two playgrounds with fresh paint and a thick layer of pea gravel, hauled bit by bit in wheelbarrows from a distant pile.

We painted the cafeteria kitchen, installed new stainless steel counters and shelves, and replaced two screen walls.

Joyce Ellis, the principal of the school, who was our guest here back in October when plans were being made for this trip, invited me into her office the final afternoon of our work. She was deeply grateful for our efforts, and more keenly grateful for the fact that there are people in this world who will spend their own money and take their vacation time to work for the betterment of others.

In a meeting with her shortly before we boarded the bus to leave for the final time, she said, "Tell the good people of Trinity when you return home that you all have touched us deeply. We have seen God in you. And be sure to thank them for giving us so much!"

From listening and watching our group throughout the week, I knew that they received a sense of gratitude and appreciation without any words being spoken. Since returning home and reading the evaluations, I know that many of them experienced an intersection of faith and life in new ways.

The presence of God in their work was clearly evident. For some, this new experience of joining with others in a mission trip was life changing. There is already great enthusiasm to go back again next year. Yes, we'll be back next year and you're invited to join us.

Some people may wonder why we went all the way to Jamaica to do this sort of thing. That's a good question to raise. Not to diminish the fine mission work that Trinity does right in our own community through our efforts in things like the Interfaith Hospitality Network, The Community Table, the Red Cross Bloodmobile and Hmong Refugee resettlement work, Mission Jamaica has added a global sense to the Christian community of which we are a part.

Several people learned during the week that people are the same wherever they go - human need and the importance of sharing doesn't have a border.

There's a second response to the question, "Why take a group of people all the way to Jamaica to do a mission project?" The experience of working on a common goal within a Christian community of volunteers in a setting far from home, and far different from home, has a way of developing a greater sense of serving, and that is not quickly diminished when the trip is over.

In other words, I know that many of the people who were with us last week will continue on to be greater servants here, and for the rest of their lives. They formed relationships with each other, and experienced God in a different way that will impact this congregation for a long time to come.

I'm most thankful that our congregation joined in this Mission Jamaica effort. Your contributions of money and goods was used directly in our efforts at Hope Valley school. Your support in spirit and prayer was something the group recalled each day and we included you in our prayers.

I believe God was at work to bring about something new for us in this mission; and I saw it happen time and time again in the months leading up to our trip as well as during the trip itself.

For some people who were with us in Jamaica, life will not be the same now. God has changed them through this experience. Do you know why I know this? God was at work last week, and when God is present, things change.

"Do not remember the former things, or consider the things of old. I am about to do a new thing."

The word of the Lord from Isaiah this morning tells us about change - about a God who is always moving us into the future.

The God you have come to worship today is a God who is always creating. This God loves to create! "I am about to do a new thing," God says. "Don't you perceive it?"

For the people of Israel to whom these words were first spoken, the intent was to encourage and give hope. These are the folks, you might remember, that God led forth from slavery in Egypt. Through the Red Sea, God guided them into freedom.

It wasn't long after these people gained their freedom that they began to mumble. They whined about how much better the good old days of slavery in Egypt were where life was safe and predictable.

Can you imagine how God took to that? So God gives them a new word. "Forget about the past you people, I don't want to hear any more of it! Quit your whining. I'm about to do a new thing. Open your eyes and be ready!"

Now, do you know people today who whine about the present and long for the good old days?

Do you like the fact that God says to let go of the past and get ready for something new? Don't even think of the past? That has to rub you a bit. Our history is important to us! We spend a lot more time celebrating our remembrances of the past than we do anticipating and welcoming the future!

So I would guess that these words of God, "**Do not remember the former things, or consider the things of old. I am about to do a new thing,"** are tough for us to take.

They are tough because to forget and move forward demands that we let go of the past and trust in a God who has promised to do wonderful new things in our lives.

If you've ever been around a kid who feels his or her expectations have been shortchanged, you've heard the words, "but you promised."

"But you promised to buy me that Beanie Baby if I cleaned my room."

I think we all have "but you promised lists," no matter what our age.

To move into God's future and trust that God is going to bring about something new, requires us to let go of our "but you promised" lists.

What's on your "but you promised" list?

*But you promised that my parents would never let me down. You owe me!

*But you promised that my children would appreciate the sacrifices I made, that they would repay me by looking after me in my old age. You owe me.

*But you promised that if I didn't abuse my body with chemicals or drugs, if I exercised and ate properly, I wouldn't' get cancer. You promised!

*But you promised that children outlive their parents, that the old die first. You owe me.

*But you promised that marriage was forever.

*But you promised....

"Do not remember the former things, or consider the things of old. I am about to do a new thing."

To follow a God who is about to do a new thing means we need to trust that this God has our best interests at heart. God does! Look through the Bible!

God led the people of Israel out of slavery and into a new land, not because God was tired of hearing their whining, but because God had chosen them to be his people. It was out of love that God led them and told them to let go of the past and get ready for the future. The same is true for us.

Have some fun in the coming days, perceiving the new things that God is doing in this world, in this church, in your life.

If you doubt me - that God is doing new things. If you just can't accept the fact that God is calling you to let go of the past, and move into something new, just look at that cross.

It was a terrible, awful and depressing Friday afternoon when some people took Jesus' body down from the cross.

But it was a predictable and familiar day in Jerusalem. The people who watched Jesus die that Friday afternoon had all seen crucifixions before and they knew what they meant.

But they probably couldn't conceive of God's words, "**Do not remember the former things, or consider the things of old. I am about to do a new thing.**"

Easter morning is the greatest evidence we have that God delights in doing new things. I hope you perceive it!

Amen.

***

Five Loaves and Two Fish

August 1, 1999

Pentecost 10/A

Matthew 14: 13-21

Now when Jesus heard this, he withdrew from there in a boat to a deserted place by himself. But when the crowds heard it, they followed him on foot from the towns. When he went ashore, he saw a great crowd; and he had compassion for them and cured their sick. When it was evening, the disciples came to him and said, 'This is a deserted place, and the hour is now late; send the crowds away so that they may go into the villages and buy food for themselves.' Jesus said to them, 'They need not go away; you give them something to eat.'

They replied, 'We have nothing here but five loaves and two fish.' And he said, 'Bring them here to me.' Then he ordered the crowds to sit down on the grass. Taking the five loaves and the two fish, he looked up to heaven, and blessed and broke the loaves, and gave them to the disciples, and the disciples gave them to the crowds. And all ate and were filled; and they took up what was left over of the broken pieces, twelve baskets full. And those who ate were about five thousand men, besides women and children.

Dear Friends,

When people feel overwhelmed, what are common phrases they utter?

"I'm up to my eyeballs."

"I'm at wits end."

"I just can't take this anymore."

Today's Bible reading has a phrase which you and I have probably never spoken in response to feeling overwhelmed by circumstances around us, "We have no more than five loaves and two fish."

"We have no more than five loaves and two fish." It is the response of the parent worried about her child. Children today face so many pressures at school with their peers. There are so many influences, so many temptations children face today. What are we parents to do?

"We have no more than five loaves and two fish." It is the response of the small business owner struggling to find and keep good employees in a robust economy. How can he compete with the big chain discount store that has just opened on the edge of town that offers more money and benefits? After all, the small business owner has "no more than five loaves and two fish."

It is the response of the ecologist who watches our air and water die a slow, lingering death but can never afford to mount much of a campaign in Madison or Washington. The people who can afford to get an ear in those places are the lobbyists for huge industries which keep belching their toxic smoke into the sky and emptying their poison wastes into our streams. What are we to do?

"We have no more than five loaves and two fish." It is the response of the spouse who is desperately trying to bring life in a dying marriage, and who grows weary of being the only partner working at the relationship.

"We have no more than five loaves and two fish." It is the response of the student who finds life on campus so demanding that he or she no longer knows how to cope and considers destructive alternatives.

"We have no more than five loaves and two fish." It is the response of the employee whose boss never has a kind or encouraging word. But how can you quit when your pension is tied up in the company and you don't want to move and lose seniority?

"We have no more than five loaves and two fish." It is the response all of us sometimes offer when life seems larger than our resources are to deal with it.

"We have no more than five loaves and two fish." What are we to do?

Certainly, that was the response of the disciples when a huge crowd followed Jesus into the wilderness near Bethsaida. The Bible says five thousand men (plus women and children).

You and I know, of course, that is a sexist way of taking attendance. But the authors of the Bible in centuries past did not know that. It was just their way of counting heads. "Five thousand men plus women and children" probably put the crowd at a number closer to 20,000. That's a lot of mouths to feed.

These people had come to listen to Jesus' words, to feel his healing touch bringing their broken lives back to wholeness. Now, the Bible says, the hour had grown late and the crowd was hungry. There was no way to buy food for so many people. It would have taken bags of money to buy enough food - the equivalent of eight month's pay. Surely the disciples didn't have that much money. Even if they did, the stores were closed, and fast food places hadn't been invented yet.

So when the disciples went to Jesus and suggested He send the crowds away so they could eat their bread and fish without looking selfish, Jesus said to them, "They need not go away; you give them something to eat."

Well, there's the rub, isn't it? Jesus is always asking more of us than we have to give, as spouses and parents and workers and on and on.

Jesus calls us to love, even when loving is difficult. Jesus calls us to forgive, even when we have been wronged. Jesus calls us to witness, even when we may be laughed at. To stand fast and firm on our principles, even when it means standing alone.

Those things aren't easy to do. After all, we are not Jesus! Our powers are limited! "We have no more than five loaves and two fish."

Fortunately for the disciples and for us, the story doesn't end there (with Jesus asking the impossible of the disciples), *"You give them something to eat,"* he said.

The disciples answered, *"How? We have no more than five loaves and two fish."*

Then Jesus said softly, *"Bring them here to me."*

Then he "*blessed the loaves and fish, gave them to the disciples, and the disciples gave them to the crowds."* And what happened?

"And all ate and were satisfied, and they took up what was left over... twelve baskets full." In the midst of feeling inadequate, the disciples fed 20,000 people and there were leftovers!

There's the good news for you moms and dads who find yourselves wondering, "Do I have what it takes to parent these kids?" The answer is "no," we don't have what it takes. At best, in the face of overwhelming odds, *"we have no more than five loaves and two fish."*

We have a God who whispers, "Bring them to me. Bring to me your skills and weaknesses as parents; your strengths and fears, your children and their futures. Bring them to me, and I will make you adequate for the task at hand."

There's the good news for spouses in troubled marriages facing great challenges.

For students who always feel as though they are swimming up-stream.

For people of conscience who feel called to take a risky stance on some public issue. What is one person against city hall, anyway?

When accompanied by Jesus, one person can be a majority.

Jesus says to all, "Bring them to me:" your hopes, dreams and convictions.

"Bring them to me:" your burdens, challenges and responsibilities.

For he who took five loaves of bread and two fish from the lunch bag of disciples and fed 20,000 can do it again, even with the meager resources in our lunch bags.

When life gets the best of us, perhaps it is because we focus too much on how little we can do and too little on how much Jesus can do.

Earlier this summer, I was together with a couple of friends from my seminary days, helping one of them move. David and his wife recently purchased a home at a lovely spot on a lake in Minnesota. The three of us timed our visit to coincide with moving.

David has always been known to utilize his friends in constructive ways! Moving in to this new home turned out to be more of a challenge than we anticipated.

On Friday evening, standing with two other pastors, we surrounded a computer desk, trying to use our collective wisdom to determine how to assemble it and attach the movable keyboard drawer. At one point, Julie came into the room. Julie is David's twelve-year-old daughter.

Julie joined her mother who was standing in the doorway, observing the three of us as we impersonated furniture assemblers. After a few minutes, Julie turned to her mom and said, "How many Lutheran pastors does it take ...?"

We were not amused. Eventually, Mary rescued us from the project by luring us away with bowls of ice cream. Once she had us in the kitchen, she offered some sound advice, "Call someone who knows what to do!"

The truth is, I can't always assemble the furniture or attach the drawers alone. I can't always heal the broken hearts or open the closed minds or change the unfair systems or right the wrongs or raise the kids or love the unlovely all by myself. Can you?

Instead, in the face of those challenges (and a thousand others like them), I find myself throwing up my hands in despair and saying, "What am I supposed to do? I have no more than five loaves of bread and two fish!"

But, what I do have (and what we all have), is the freedom to call on a God of abundance who knows what to do.

When life seems too big and I feel too small, our God is there and God can do what I cannot. God can right the wrongs and heal the hurts and love the unlovely and guide the children. God can take my paltry little handful of bread and fish and turn it into a feast.

However little I may possess in terms of talent or resources, Jesus whispers, "Bring them to me," and with Him, my little becomes a lot.

"Bring them to me." Those words comprise the antidote when we feel small, ill-equipped or overwhelmed by the tasks that lie before us.

"Bring them to me," Jesus says, "and I will make you more than adequate for life as you find it."

Amen.

***

The Adventure of Grace

August 29, 1999

Pentecost 14/A

Matthew 16:24-26

Then Jesus told his disciples, "If any want to become my followers, let them deny themselves and take up their cross and follow me. For those who want to save their life will lose it, and those who lose their life for my sake will find it. For what will it profit them if they gain the whole world but forfeit their life? Or what will they give in return for their life?"

Dear Friends,

Last weekend, I returned from a trip to Alaska. It was a spectacular adventure to a land of unspoiled, unending beauty and richness. Several times during the trip, I was struck by the majesty of the land and the creative hand of our God. I also marveled at how we as human beings are gifted by such grandeur and how we fit in the creative work of God.

The words of Psalm 8 came to mind more than once: *"When I look at your heavens, the work of your fingers, the moon and the stars that you have established; what are human beings that you are mindful of them, mortals that you care for them?"*

One afternoon of this trip, I went on a four-hour, white-water rafting adventure on a glacier fed stream. I say, "adventure," because the final canyon on this river is a Class V rapids. The

American Whitewater Affiliation classifies water levels and describes Class V as, "very violent rapids and drops which may contain large, unavoidable waves, holes, or steep chutes. Swims are dangerous and self-rescue difficult."

Before we began, the guides outfitted us in dry suits, life-vests and helmets. I'd never been covered from head to toe with such thick, tight-fitting, floatation materials.

Once we arrived beside the stream, the raft was unloaded and the guide shared safety instructions. We were told of paddling commands and shown how to paddle. Then our guide briefed us on the various ways we could drown, be injured or otherwise tortured by the power of the river.

Water is nothing to mess with! As the safety lecture came to a close, we were required to do a little swim test - enacting the self-rescue techniques we had been taught. I was the final one in the water - perhaps that gives you a clue as to my courage level.

Really, after that safety lecture, I was beginning to feel the pins and needles under that rubber skin! The swim test went well, and immediately I felt myself relaxing and returning to a pleasant level of anticipation of an adventure I had looked forward to for some time.

At the first rapids, Todd, the guy in the front of the raft, fell out. After a minute he was rescued and we continued without incident through the first and second canyons. They were the training waters for the final, Class V violent rapids. Throughout the afternoon our guide encouraged, directed and relaxed us and always, always reminded us of safety tips.

As we approached the final canyon and the Class V rapids, my blood was pulsing quickly. The scenery, which was outstanding along every inch of this river, suddenly became imperceptible, drowned out by the sight and sound of the approaching rushing water and the guide's preparatory instructions.

A rescue raft joined us just before the wicked rapids commenced - piloted by a single, skilled man. Another rescuer was stationed on a rock cliff jutting out high above the churning water. He was armed with two rescue ropes. We were informed as to their procedures; in case something went wrong in the rapids.

Our final approach to this canyon didn't go quite as planned. As we came to the first and most challenging rapids, called the "suck hole" for its hydraulic like down-moving clutches, the chute was just wide enough for the raft to pass.

However, a car-sized rock split the rushing water and a current thrust us to the left. Throwing the raft sideways along the rock, we began tipping right into the demonically churning waters. Almost capsizing, two men on the right plunged into the menacing suck hole.

Our guide leaped to the opposite side, prostrating himself over the edge to stabilize the raft. The rescue boat and man on shore sprang into action. Two ropes flew onto the water and the rescue raft descended upon us. One fellow rafter in the water immediately began his self-rescue procedure. The other was gripped by the hydraulic undertow of the waters, as was our raft. The guide was shouting commands now!

The remaining four of us in the raft followed them as well as we could - thrusting our paddles into the storming water. Eventually, we overcame the downward pull of the rapids and freed our raft. The powerful clutches of the water and movement of the raft released the still floundering man, and together we floated into calmer waters. The exhilaration, excitement and safe conclusion to my first white-water rafting adventure is an experience I won't soon forget. I look forward to the next one.

Have you ever had a really good adventure? Although I've faced many challenges, I can honestly say this was one of the best ones of my life.

That trip reminded me once again that you and I are wired for adventure. God has placed deep down in our hearts a yearning for newness, a break in the routine, a dash to the edge. That's why we stand in line for the latest Star Wars movie. That's why we spend big bucks to fly to Disneyworld. That's why we ride rollercoasters or waterslides. That's why a person throws off the tie or business suit, dons a leather jacket, hops on a Harley Davidson, and rides to Sturgis, South Dakota for a motorcycle rally. Go figure! The need for adventure!

When wise and learned elders are asked, "If you could live your life all over again, what would you do differently?" They respond hands down, "I'd take more risks."

God has wired us for adventure. And today's Bible reading from Matthew is the launching point.

Two thousand years ago, a young man roamed the dusty roads of Galilee inviting people to join him. This was nothing unique. Many leaders at that time invited people to join them. "Follow my teaching," they would say. Or, "follow my political agenda,' they would say.

But this man, this Jesus, spoke something so unique when he said, "Follow me."

Follow me! Now why would these people leave their homes to follow Jesus? Why would Peter drop his nets and leave his fishing business? Why would

Matthew throw away his lucrative tax collecting business? Why would Mary leave? Why would all these people leave the comforts of home, family, friends and security of jobs to follow Jesus? What captured their hearts? What motivated them to sell all and give all to follow Jesus?

Jesus invited them to an adventure. Not just any adventure. Not an economic adventure. Not a political one. Jesus invited them to an adventure of grace. Think about it. Jesus healed people. He taught how to make life meaningful. He lifted people's burdens. Jesus welcomed people and his message and actions were a ministry of grace.

Grandpa went to visit little Josh, his grandson one beautiful fall afternoon. But just before Grandpa arrived, Josh did something he knew was wrong and so was suffering the consequences, and was sent to his room for a time. Josh didn't like it - but he followed his mom's orders.

The doorbell rang and Grandpa came in. Josh could hear this from his room. "Where's Josh," asked Grandpa.

"In his room," his mother replied as she told her dad about the little incident which resulted in the time-out.

Grandpa, having come specifically to play with Josh, faced a dilemma. He wanted desperately to be with Josh and hold him tight. Yet ,he knew a rule was rule and had to be obeyed. A few minutes later, after Mom had gone into the kitchen to make some lemonade, she walked down the hallway and noticed Josh's door was ajar. Peeking in, she found Grandpa and Josh laying side-by-side on the bed quietly talking to each other.

Two thousand years ago, God so desperately wanted to be with you and me that he sent his Son Jesus into our world, to live with us, to become one of us, to understand us and to know our joys and pains. God wanted to live with us in every way we experience this life. But not only did he live life with us, he literally gave his life for us.

Queen Victoria had a very ill daughter named Alice. She grew up with illness and lived her adult years with illness, too. Yet Alice married and had children. Tragically, her son contracted diphtheria and eventually died from the disease.

But while her son was ill, the doctors told Alice that she could not come near him, lest she contract the disease and die as well. For weeks Alice watched her son from a distance as the nurses tended to him, fed him, put him to bed. One night Alice overheard her son say as he was being tucked into bed, "Why doesn't mommy kiss me goodnight? Mommy used to always come and kiss me goodnight? Why doesn't she do that anymore?"

Alice's heart broke. She raced to her son, picking him up, and she hugged and kissed him.

Four weeks later, Alice and her son were buried together. Not only did God send his son to live with us, but he sent his son to die for us. Jesus came to love us, forgive us, heal us...and when we could not accept this grace, he was killed. But he rose from the dead.

The victorious Jesus is the same One who says, "Follow me. Follow **me.**"

Now imagine if you were Peter or Matthew or one of those disciples hearing the words of Jesus today: "*If any want to become my followers, let them deny themselves and take up their cross and follow me.*" Boy, even for us, they're shocking instructions Jesus gives. Imagine the responses Jesus got:

Jesus, you want me to deny myself? Deny my pleasures? My joys? My own goals? You want me to take up my cross? You want me to go through whatever suffering may come from following you? Oh, Jesus, if you want to hear about suffering, I'll tell you about **my** cross...my work is my cross, Lord.

Or, My spouse, that's my cross. My mother-in-law, she's my cross!

But Jesus says, "No, no, no. I'm not asking you to suffer...I'm asking you to die. Not physical death. But to die to your own efforts, your own wants. Die to the idea that you can make your own way in this life."

You see, when Matthew wrote these words of Jesus about 85 A.D. Christians were being persecuted in a big way. If you claimed to be a Christian, the government leaders might chop off your head. They might burn you at the stake or nail you to a cross.

So Matthew says, "What would it benefit you if you gave up your faith and lost true life?"

Jesus invites us today to make an exchange. He says, "Let's exchange your self-reliance for my guidance. Let's exchange your hurt for my healing. Let's exchange your best efforts to please God for my unconditional acceptance. Let's make an exchange."

My friends, to deny yourself and to take your cross - it is to let Jesus Christ be the center of your life.

Jesus invites us today to the adventure of life. It means we can step out of our comfort zone to follow - to make this exchange. There's some scariness and there are some possible dangers - just like my rafting experience. But it's an adventure, too! To step out and follow Jesus is an adventure where God's grace is always present.

A middle-aged man shared with me his attempt to provide security for his family. He said, "I worked so hard to provide for my family and myself, but in the process I've lost it all. I've lost my children - they don't know me and I don't know them. And I've lost my wife."

Jesus asks us, "*What does it profit us if we gain the whole world but lose our life?*"

Jesus invites us to something great. He says, "Let go of everything and step out into the adventure of following me. I'll be with you and you will have life abundant."

"Follow me." It is the adventure of grace.

Amen.

***

Here I Am, Send Me

June 18, 2000

Isaiah 6:1-8

In the year that King Uzziah died, I saw the Lord sitting on a throne, high and lofty; and the hem of his robe filled the temple. Seraphs were in attendance above him; each had six wings: with two they covered their faces, and with two they covered their feet, and with two they flew. And one called to another and said:

'Holy, holy, holy is the Lord of hosts;
the whole earth is full of his glory.'

The pivots on the thresholds shook at the voices of those who called, and the house filled with smoke. And I said: 'Woe is me! I am lost, for I am a man of unclean lips, and I live among a people of unclean lips; yet my eyes have seen the King, the Lord of hosts!'

Then one of the seraphs flew to me, holding a live coal that had been taken from the altar with a pair of tongs. The seraph touched my mouth with it and said: 'Now that this has touched your lips, your guilt has departed and your sin is blotted out.' Then I heard the voice of the Lord saying, 'Whom shall I send, and who will go for us?' And I said, 'Here am I; send me!'

Dear Friends;

Last summer, the tragic and untimely death of John F. Kennedy, Jr., caused many Americans to recall the all-too-familiar details of the death of his father, President John F. Kennedy, 36 years earlier. Once again we watched another of the all-too-familiar tragedies unfold for the Kennedys.

The media, always taken by this family, asked the question, "Is this the end of Camelot?" referring to the time of idealized beauty and charmed living, as we seem to remember during Jack and Jackie's years in the White House.

At age 38, JFK, Jr., had attained Camelot-like greatness reminiscent of his parents. In some ways the Kennedy's, have been this country's royalty and John Jr. was the prince. His death, like the death of his father, was another blow to many.

During the days after Kennedy's plane disappeared in the Atlantic, we saw many images on television. Ships and helicopters scanning the ocean surface for signs of wreckage. Vacationers lining the beaches watching for any sign of hope. We saw the Kennedy family, gathered at Aunt Ethel's house seeking support and solace in one another.

When tragedy strikes, most people have a natural tendency to seek God. Last summer the media widely reported the fact that the Kennedy family held Mass every morning as they awaited news about JFK Jr., his wife and sister-in-law.

Tragically, though, it seems that few persons are successful in their quest to "find God" in the midst of tragedy and trauma. Far fewer follow through and serve the God whom they find in tumultuous circumstances.

In times of crisis, we turn our attention heavenward and ask, "Why?"

Yet it seems that we never pause long enough to hear God answer that question.

What happens when crisis comes into your life? What happens when your version of "Camelot" is ripped away?

The Bible reading today from Isaiah tells us about a Camelot of biblical times that suddenly ends. It tells us about a person who comes through the tragedy believing and serving God.

This is the story of Isaiah when he was a young man. He lived in the nation of Judah. During those days, Judah was enjoying a "Camelot" of sorts. Under the reign of King Uzziah, the nation was experiencing prosperity, unity, peace, and a general sense that life had become ideal.

Yet, unbeknown to them, the people would soon be forced to cope with "the collapse of Camelot."

Uzziah became king in at the age of sixteen, following in the footsteps of his father, who had been removed from the throne.

Other books of the Bible tell us that the people loved Uzziah (2 Kings 4:21), and they were thrilled when he became king. During his reign, Judah saw a time of great military and economic prosperity. Uzziah accomplished these goals while being obedient to God, the Bible tells us (2 Kings 15:3).

Judah's version of "Camelot" collapsed, just as suddenly and tragically as did the Kennedy's when King Uzziah made one tragic and serious mistake.

According to the Bible, (2 Chronicles 26) Uzziah made the ill-fated, prideful decision to personally offer incense in the Temple, even though the Law of the Lord clearly stated that only (the Levitical) priests were permitted to make such offerings.

As a result of his disobedience, the Lord allowed Uzziah to be stricken with fatal leprosy (2 Kings 15:5). Physically unable to continue as King, Uzziah had no choice but to leave the throne. When he died as a leper, he was not even buried in the Royal Tombs. (2 Chronicles 26:23).

This was a terrible time for the people of Judah. No doubt the fall of their beloved king caused a collective and individual period of grieving.

In our lives, many of us have or will experience personal tragedies which occur in a split-second, no-warning fashion. The sudden death of a loved one ... the surprising, inexplicable loss of a job ... a spouse who ups and leaves ... or a seemingly nonstop chain of crises ...

There are many things that can cause our personal "Camelots" to tumble and collapse. One minute, everything is "smooth sailing." The next minute, it is clear that life will never be the same again.

Back to the Bible reading again, young Isaiah is in just this sort of situation. He loved King Uzziah and was deeply troubled by his fall from the throne and subsequent death. The test for Isaiah was to believe in a God of love and follow and serve that God, even in the midst of loss and grief.

The Bible reading tells us that Isaiah does more than mourn. He does more than sentimentalize the life and memory of Uzziah. Isaiah moves forward, in response to God.

You see, whenever tragedy comes into human life, whenever we are grieving or mourning some loss, God never stops leading, guiding, and sending us. God does not put our mission of serving "on hold" when life gets difficult. Why? Because God knows that we are best able to cope with difficult times if we keep on following and serving Him.

Again, the bible reading teaches us: When Isaiah was caught up in the despair over losing Uzziah, God remained active in his life. The Bible is clear to tell us:

-It is God who reveals Himself to Isaiah - Isaiah didn't go searching for God;

-it is God who makes known heaven's glory through those angels singing "Holy, Holy, Holy" to pick Isaiah up;

-it is God who makes it possible for Isaiah to stand up and respond;

-it is God who extends the specific call to Isaiah to serve Him.

And what does Isaiah have to do in the midst of his grief? All he has to do is look, listen, and respond!

When life is dark and difficult for us, that's really all God requires of you and me as well.

- Look, see what God is doing.
- Listen and hear what God is saying.
- Respond, go where God is directing. God will take care of the rest!

No matter how bad you're hurting or grieving, no matter how drained your emotional batteries, God comes to you like God came to Isaiah and calls you to follow.

I love this Bible reading because Isaiah does something I often don't do very well, and Isaiah reminds me to do it. He listens to God. He humbles himself before the Lord and hears God's instructions.

You see, it is precisely because Isaiah took time to listen for God's voice (and because God was, of course, faithful to speak!), that Isaiah does not even consider for a moment the possibility that God has "forgotten" him!

In crisis situations, sometimes we feel that God has forgotten us. Maybe that's because we've not listened for God's voice.

I visited Emma Mae one summer day back in 1986. Emma Mae's husband had died suddenly and tragically nine months earlier. After the funeral, Emma Mae went home, turned down all the blinds, closed the doors and stayed in her house, full of grief and despair.

For nine months, she didn't answer her phone, didn't welcome her friends who came to comfort her. She didn't come to worship and claim her place in the community of faith of which she had been a participant for decades.

Instead Emma Mae shut herself off from her friends, her church, her God. Emma Mae lived with the notion that God ought to do all the work when she was grieving, that God ought to come and find her in the valley, pick her up, dust her off, pat her head, and wash all her woes away. Emma Mae was convinced God had forgotten her.

When I visited Emma Mae that afternoon, I listened to her story and listened intently to her grief. Then we prayed together. In our praying we listened for God, and we remembered the stories of God coming to people in the midst of their grief.

After we prayed, together we spoke the familiar words of the 23rd Psalm, "*... though I walk through the valley of death.*"

You've heard those words. Emma Mae had recited them hundreds of times. But on this day that one phrase struck her directly. Psalm 23 doesn't speak of sitting in the valley of death, with the blinds drawn and the door closed, waiting passively for God's rescue. Rather we WALK through the valley.

Maybe that's why God, in all God's great wisdom, expects us to take some action -- like God asked of Isaiah. In his grief, God came to Isaiah, called him to follow and serve God. In the same way, God will rescue and deliver us in our trials, but God wants us to avail ourselves of that rescue by continuing to look, listen and obey Him.

Well, good old Isaiah listened and obeyed God. Even though life had dealt his nation a blow, Isaiah remained steadfastly willing to serve God, and he placed no limitations on that service.

"Here I am, send me," he said.

When crisis comes your way, when life seems to collapse, keep serving God. Keep listening for God. Keep worshiping God. Keep responding to God.

If you sit back and say, "God, when [if?] everything gets better, or calms down, I'll serve You again," chances are great that you'll never actually do it.

Why? Because it's not likely that things will ever "get better" or "calm down," until you begin to serve Him again!

Whatever life deals you today or tomorrow, resolve now that you will remain steadfast in your service to, and worship of, the God of all grace and goodness, and like Isaiah respond, "Here I am, send me."

Amen.

***

The Verdict

June 16, 2002

Pentecost 4A

Romans 5:1-8

Therefore, since we are justified by faith, we have peace with God through our Lord Jesus Christ, through whom we have obtained access to this grace in which we stand; and we boast in our hope of sharing the glory of God. And not only that, but we also boast in our sufferings, knowing that suffering produces endurance, and endurance produces character, and character produces hope, and hope does not disappoint us, because God's love has been poured into our hearts through the Holy Spirit that has been given to us.

For while we were still weak, at the right time Christ died for the ungodly. Indeed, rarely will anyone die for a righteous person - though perhaps for a good person someone might actually dare to die. But God proves his love for us in that while we still were sinners Christ died for us.

Dear Friends,

Last fall, I was called to jury duty. This is the second time in the 14 years that I've lived here that this duty of citizenship has been put upon me. The first time, back in 1991, I missed the opportunity to be seated on a jury, but not this last time.

Thanks to television shows, movies and John Grisham novels, many people have a notion of what courtroom activity and jury-work entails. I appreciated the chance to see firsthand the real-life portrayal of the work of the court. I found it to be quite enlightening and engaging and I will gladly serve again if the opportunity arises. Just a little aside though, if you're called for jury duty, bring a novel or a magazine. There's plenty of down time!

The case this jury would decide was a criminal case regarding the darker side of human nature: child enticement and sex with a minor.

After the initial public questioning of the jury panel, eight candidates were struck, as is the normal course of jury selection. Because the parties in this case involved people of different races, the attorneys and judge were very intent upon screening the remaining 12 potential jurors for racial bias.

We each had a final step to proceed through before the jury would be seated. To provide for confidentiality, each jury candidate was interviewed privately in the judge's chambers. Wow, not only did I see the workings of the courtroom, I got to the see inner sanctum!

One by one, each of the 12 potential jurors filed into the chambers. This is where the magazine or novel came in handy. For nearly two hours, we waited for the process to conclude. Three times, the judge, attorneys and court reporter moved from courtroom to chambers as, for various untold reasons, potential jurors were dismissed following the private questioning. Finally, at high noon, the jury was seated and the judge informed us of our responsibility and what we would weigh and decide upon before we'd depart for home in the darkness of a beautiful fall evening. Then, the hour-and-a-half lunch break commenced! Again, bring a novel or magazine.

The process of presenting evidence and questioning witnesses lasted about 3 hours, and was interspersed with breaks where we were filed back into the windowless jury room to wait. We were regularly instructed that we could not discuss anything about the case during these breaks. Making small talk with 11 strangers gets a little tedious after a couple hours.

By 6pm, the closing arguments had been given; the judge gave us our instructions, and we filed back into that windowless room. It was now up to us to come back with a verdict. Guilty? Not guilty? Two charges - with verdicts on each count needed.

After a quick pizza dinner, I was selected to be the jury foreperson and we proceeded to debate the trial. It wasn't long into the deliberations that it became apparent that, on the first charge, we were of one mind: guilty. The defense attorney even granted that verdict in his closing statement.

But reaching a verdict on the other charge of child enticement would prove to be much more challenging. We took a straw vote and the jury was almost evenly split. There were jurors on each side quite adamant in their position. Discussion ensued and within a couple of minutes, words were spoken between two men on opposite sides of the verdict - words which were less than constructive.

One juror felt his position was being attacked on personal grounds. We were quickly heading down a troublesome path, where lack of respect, personal disregard and unhelpful emotion would prolong the task before us.

Now, at this point as the foreperson, I didn't want a hung jury! What was needed to bring this jury back to the task of reaching a verdict was a return to the guiding documents, in this case, the law.

Thanks to the fine work and leadership of Judge Proctor, we had in our hands excerpts from Wisconsin law code on child enticement. Going back to that document and carefully reading and thinking through each word helped short-circuit the fray and focus our deliberation.

Another straw vote was taken. 11-1 in favor of a verdict. The sole hold-out was adamant that he could not with good conscience change his vote. Perhaps coincidentally, this was the same juror who earlier felt he was being attacked on personal grounds for his position. It was at this point, that group dynamics began to really come to bear. Several different jurors addressed this man with perspective of how the law regarding child enticement applied to this case. After nearly 30 minutes of discussion and repeated review of the law, it became obvious that this juror was not going to be convinced by the 11 others. He wanted more explanation of the law than we had before us. He wanted to hear the judge's word on interpretation of the law, and his alone.

So we prepared a written question for the judge and gave it to the bailiff. It was only a matter of minutes and Judge Proctor responded. *"I've given you all the direction I can,"* he wrote. *"Go back to the law and decide the case on its merits and the testimony you heard."* Those were his only words.

My friends, today's Bible reading from Romans has a word from the judge. Romans was written by a man named Paul to young Christian churches not long after the resurrection of Jesus. Paul uses the language of the courtroom to talk about people's relationship to God. The Bible reading says God has declared a verdict upon us.

Think of all the verdicts we declare upon others. Sometimes our verdicts directly impact other people and sometimes change the course of their lives forever. The verdicts follow all stages of life:

-I've decided not to go to college.

-I've decided I will marry you.

-I've decided I don't want to have a baby.

-I've decided to hire you. I've decided to fire you.

-I've decided I can't forgive you.

-I've decided not to go through any more treatment.

-I've decided I don't love you.

We cast all kinds of verdicts. Our verdicts are rarely based on law. Rather, our verdicts are based upon what others have done that's angered or hurt us or upon what they haven't done that we wish they would do.

Imagine the list of things we've done or not done on which God could declare a verdict concerning us?

Have you ever dishonored God's name? Have you ever done something that you wish you hadn't done? Have you had a thought that you are not proud of having? Have you left a kind or encouraging word unspoken? Have you failed to help a friend in need? Have you neglected feeding the hungry, housing the homeless, visiting those who are sick and in prison? Have you ever failed to share your food and money with people in need? Have you refused to forgive someone? If you answered "yes" to any of those questions, then God has every right to declare you GUILTY.

This Bible reading from Romans begins with an easily overlooked opening phrase which says: **"Since we are justified by faith,"** or in other words, *since God declares us not guilty of all our* *sin,* we have peace with God. Despite our obvious guilt, God says, "*I declare you not guilty.*"

And we ask, "Why? I know I'm guilty. Why this verdict, God?"

And God says, "*I gave my Son, Jesus, to show you how much I love and forgive you. When it comes to the verdict on your sin, He paid the price for you. Because of Jesus, even though there is ample evidence to convict you, I declare you not guilty.*"

It took only a few more minutes of deliberation following Judge Proctor's response to the jury that the one juror yielded. The jury had reached a verdict.

I knocked on the door of the jury room and the bailiff passed the word to the judge that the jury was in. I completed the two forms indicating our verdict and signed them. It wasn't long and the jury filed back into the courtroom. We were seated, and as foreperson, my seat was now the first in the jury box, closest to the man upon whom our verdict would come to bear.

Judge Proctor called my name. "Mr. Jacobson, has the jury reached a verdict."

"Yes, your honor. We have."

The bailiff came and took the two pieces of paper from my hand, and walked them over to the judge. With no noticeable facial expression, he looked over our verdicts and then read them aloud: "Guilty. Guilty."

With surprising haste, the courtroom cleared. But Judge Proctor asked the jury to stay for a few minutes. He thanked us, and then debriefed the experience. Again he told us of how important we were in the exercise of justice in this country. He fielded our questions and spoke with surprising frankness. Then, he bid us "good night."

As the jury meandered down the now quiet hallway of the Eau Claire County Courthouse, about a third of the jury hung together to speak about the experience and the magnitude of what we had decided, which was now becoming clearer as we talked.

To our surprise, the defense attorney and the man we had just declared guilty came upon us and exited. Our conversation quickly halted, and we watched silently as the two men got into their cars and drove away - the defendant awaiting sentencing on our verdict, his life never to be the same.

The good news for us today is this: As you walk out of this place, the verdict is NOT GUILTY; not guilty of any of your sin. God decides and announces this verdict upon us in the hope that it will have a life-changing impact upon us right now.

We don't have to appear for sentencing. Because we are free from having to live in fear of punishment someday, we are free to, as the Bible reading says, "boast in our hope of sharing the glory of God."

Not guilty. May this verdict, given us through Jesus, be a source of joy and hope for how you live. May it be cause for sharing God's grace with everyone in your life and everyone you encounter.

Amen.

***

Trouncing Worry

October 6, 2002

Matthew 6:25-34

'Therefore I tell you, do not worry about your life, what you will eat or what you will drink, or about your body, what you will wear. Is not life more than food, and the body more than clothing? Look at the birds of the air; they neither sow nor reap nor gather into barns, and yet your heavenly Father feeds them. Are you not of more value than they? And can any of you by worrying add a single hour to your span of life? And why do you worry about clothing? Consider the lilies of the field, how they grow; they neither toil nor spin, yet I tell you, even Solomon in all his glory was not clothed like one of these. But if God so clothes the grass of the field, which is alive today and tomorrow is thrown into the oven, will he not much more clothe you—you of little faith? Therefore do not worry, saying, "What will we eat?" or "What will we drink?" or "What will we wear?" For it is the Gentiles who strive for all these things; and indeed your heavenly Father knows that you need all these things. But strive first for the kingdom of God and his righteousness, and all these things will be given to you as well.

'So do not worry about tomorrow, for tomorrow will bring worries of its own. Today's trouble is enough for today.

Dear Friends,

One weekend, a young woman brought her boyfriend home to meet her parents. This was the first visit home since this relationship had budded and become quite serious. Being the good hosts, Mom and Dad prepared a fine dinner and engaged in pleasantries throughout the meal.

Suspecting that this young man might become his son-in-law, after dinner, Dad asked him into his study for a private conversation.

"What are your plans for a career, son?" the dutiful father inquired.

"I'm a student of theology," the young man replied.

"Well, that's admirable! But what will you do to provide for yourself and a family someday?"

"I will study, and God will provide," the young man explained.

"How will you pay for the things of life?" the father continued.

"GOD will provide," said the young man, with a touch exasperation.

Seeing a path that the father didn't care to pursue at this point, the two men left the study.

At first chance, his wife caught him and asked, "How did it go?"

"Well, he has no money. He has no employment plans. But on the other hand, he thinks I'm God."

The parents spent the balance of the weekend worrying about their daughter, the relationship with this young man, and what the future might bring.

Worry. It's a common ailment of all humanity. Of all the living things God created, we humans are the only ones that worry. We worry about all sorts of things. A recent article in USA Today (September 25, 2002 - Svetlana Kolchik) summarized many things people worried about this summer.

The West Nile virus resurfaced in this country, killing a record number of people.

Children were abducted in broad daylight.

The stock market continued its slide.

Terrorism threats persisted.

Now, this fall there's even more to worry about. Almost every day, we see our president on TV trying to cheer the American public into war.

The economic news continues to get dimmer.

Yet closer to home, we always have things which cause us anxiety.

We worry about our health or the health of someone close to us.

We worry about money, fretting over stock funds and retirement accounts.

We worry about job security and our marriages.

Parents worry about children; children worry about parents.

We worry about our dress and attractiveness; some of us men worry about losing our hair.

On a spiritual level, we worry about whether our faith is strong enough, or if God really does forgive us and love us.

What are the things you worry about most?

How many of you would like to learn how to worry more? How many of you feel your life would be improved if only you could spend more time worrying?

The pressures of our daily lives and the worries that come from those pressures have a devastating effect on our health. Billions of dollars are spent each year treating anxiety.

Dr Edward Podolsky in his book *Stop Worrying and Get Well*, calls attention to the fact that worry causes heart trouble, high blood pressure, some forms of asthma, ulcers, headaches and stomach disorders.

Health care professionals say that much of what they see in their patients comes from the accumulated effects of worry and anxiety. Worrying though, is like trying to shovel smoke. It will keep you busy, wear you out, but it won't accomplish much.

Today's Bible reading stops us at the starting line of worry. Jesus says, "Don't worry! Do not worry about your life."

That seems too pat, doesn't it? Hard to swallow? Easy to dismiss. Jesus, he lived in a much simpler time, right?

Jesus dished out this advice a couple thousand years ago. That tells me that anxiety isn't a problem unique to us. Every generation has had plenty to worry about.

When Jesus said, 'Don't worry" he pointed to the sky and continued, "Look at the birds. They neither sow nor reap nor gather into barns, and yet your heavenly Father feeds them. Are you not of more value than they?"

The point, of course, is not that the birds are taken care of without work. Have you ever watched birds moving about for food? They work harder than we do! The message Jesus conveyed is that the birds do not worry about life. So if God cares for them, won't God care for you, too?

Going on, Jesus wants to trounce worry some more. He asks again, "Can any of you by worrying add a single hour to your span of life?"

If we could get Jesus to update his words for us today, he would probably add, "Worry has been proven to subtract from the length of your life, and it will diminish the quality of your life!"

Still talking to that anxious crowd, Jesus continues, "Why do you worry about clothing? Look at the wild flowers, how they grow; they don't work for clothing, but they're more beautifully dressed than royalty! So, if God provides food and clothing and life itself to birds and the flowers, will not God also provide the same for you?"

The necessities of life, the length of life, the quality of life - all things that tend to cause us anxiety.

But Jesus' message is clear: NONE of these things should particularly concern us because the God who gives us life will surely be in control of it.

After Jesus points out that our worrying is countered by God's provision for life, he sums up the problem of our anxiety in one little phrase: "you of little faith."

You see, that's what Jesus has been driving at all along. Our worrying has direct correlation to our faith.

Jesus hasn't told us that we shouldn't plan ahead. Jesus hasn't told us that we should be unconcerned about working for the things we need in life, like that young woman's boyfriend.

What Jesus wants us to remember is this: We're not in this life all by ourselves.

After he dishes out the advice not to worry about the things of life, he reminds us we have a loving God who "knows that you need these things."

This is a God who is so involved in this life with us that even the things we never think about...like providing for the birds and flowers ... are taken care of and we have nothing to do with it! If we remember that, we will not have to worry!

There's another very practical side to this whole question of worry: if we spend too much time at it, we will not have time for anything else. And that's the thrust of what Jesus says about "striving for the kingdom of God and His righteousness, and all these other things (food, clothing and so on) will be yours as well."

Think about that for a minute. If we spent all our energies worrying about our own lives, we would never begin to be concerned about anyone else. If we spent our energies worrying about our own health and the length of our own life, we would not have time to care about anyone else's health.

Jesus wants us to understand that the way to overcome our own worries is to instead be concerned, maybe even worried about others. That is what striving for the Kingdom of God is about.

One of the joys I have as a pastor is being able to watch you in a variety of activities and settings in which you serve other people. Month after month I see you serving - preparing meals for others, making quilts for others, staffing a homeless shelter for others, fixing up houses for others, giving your money for others, teaching others about faith in a gracious God, visiting others who are sick or confined.

When you do these things to care for others, I see your spirits lifted and I see your enthusiasm for life increased. At least for a while when you serve others, the worries that you carry are forgotten.

In February, a couple of dozen people from this congregation will spend several days in Kingston Jamaica on our annual mission trip.

This winter, we'll be doing something new. We'll be going into the humble, crumbling houses of people in the neighborhood of Maranatha Church - one of our global partner churches.

I was recently down there making arrangements for this trip, and had opportunity to enter one of those humble houses, which is home to a family of nine. It's basically a shack - about 10 feet by 20 feet. The roof leaks. You can see the neighbors through the holes in the walls. A bare light bulb hangs on from an exposed wire tacked to the sagging ceiling which is insulated with torn cardboard.

In a corner is a gas cooking stove which is used only when they have money to purchase the propane. The oldest daughter is a teenager, and she spends her days at home, watching television on a tiny set that's shared between several neighbors. She doesn't attend school because the family doesn't have the $75 required to enroll her in the system.

This is one family we're going to serve this winter. When we finish working there, that house will look like a palace to those folks.

It'll be another one of those times when I will see the joy in the faces and lives of those people who serve others. Without a doubt, the 20-some people from this congregation who will do this work, each have their own worries and anxieties about life. They'll bring those burdens on the plane with us to Jamaica.

I know for a fact that when we put on our work clothes and start serving our Jamaican friends, those worries and anxieties will be tempered, changed, and maybe even forgotten.

I know you can't all make a long trip like that to serve others. There are plenty of ways to serve right here at home.

One new thing we're moving toward in our new health ministry is the formation of "Care Teams." Care Team people will to do the simple things of daily life for our friends who are older or are suffering in a way which makes daily life at home difficult. A Care Team will serve by helping these folks with the basic things of life: transportation, household chores, providing a meal, simple caring friendship.

Jesus said, "*Don't worry about your life. God will take care of you. What I want you to do is strive first for the kingdom of God.*"

Jesus turns us toward other people to be concerned about their needs and in the end, our needs are answered too.

Worry is our common ailment. Jesus teaches us that it is possible to quarantine worry by making our major concern the welfare of others rather than ourselves. It's possible also, by remembering the God who loves us enough to take care of, not only our day-to-day needs, but even the needs of the birds and the flowers.

Amen.

*Edward Podolsky, M. D., Stop Worrying and Get Well, (New York: Bernard Ackerman, Inc.)

***

Angels: Fantasy or Faith

December 22, 2002

Advent 4/B

Luke 1:26-38

In the sixth month the angel Gabriel was sent by God to a town in Galilee called Nazareth, to a virgin engaged to a man whose name was Joseph, of the house of David. The virgin's name was Mary. And he came to her and said, 'Greetings, favored one! The Lord is with you.' But she was much perplexed by his words and pondered what sort of greeting this might be. The angel said to her, 'Do not be afraid, Mary, for you have found favor with God. And now, you will conceive in your womb and bear a son, and you will name him Jesus. He will be great, and will be called the Son of the Most High, and the Lord God will give to him the throne of his ancestor David. He will reign over the house of Jacob forever, and of his kingdom there will be no end.' Mary said to the angel, 'How can this be, since I am a virgin?' The angel said to her, 'The Holy Spirit will come upon you, and the power of the Most High will overshadow you; therefore the child to be born will be holy; he will be called Son of God. And now, your relative Elizabeth in her old age has also conceived a son; and this is the sixth month for her who was said to be barren. For nothing will be impossible with God.' Then Mary said, 'Here am I, the servant of the Lord; let it be with me according to your word.' Then the angel departed from her.

Dear Friends,

Some time ago at this point in December, I was visiting friends in Santa Barbara. A local church was hosting an open house to show off 450 different nativity sets from all over the world. So we went.

It was quite impressive! I found it interesting to see how the scene of Jesus' birth is envisioned by people of different cultures.

In the Russian display, Mary, Joseph and shepherds were adorned in very colorful garb. In the Mexican and Indian nativities, the characters were short and very simply dressed and their faces were brown. In one scene, which I believe was from Eastern Europe, Mary and Joseph embraced as they held baby Jesus. In another very creative depiction of the birth of Jesus, the entire nativity was carved inside half a walnut shell!

Mary, a central figure of all artistic accounts of Jesus' birth has been the focus of the beginning of our worship today. She is, without a doubt, the best known human in the nativity scene. Our Roman Catholic friends, and many of you who have ties to that tradition, know well of Mary and the song she sings as she comes to accept the life-changing role God gives in her pregnancy.

It's an angel who gives Mary a start when the announcement is made that she is pregnant with Jesus. Thus, the angel surely has an important role too. So I wonder if we should take the angel seriously or is the angel simply a dash of fantasy?

There's an old Scottish saying: "Angels can fly because they take themselves lightly." But should we take angels lightly?

In answer to that question, the Bible is of help. When angels appear in the stories of the Bible, they're shocking and frightening. What's the first things angels say when they appear to someone, *"Hey, look me over; I'm cuddly and cute."* No. They say, "*Do not be afraid!*"

There's a reason for that! Because people who see angels, are at the least surprised; at the most, scared out of their socks. This is not a normal experience; this is an experience of God.

Angels fly throughout the Bible story:

- In Genesis, the first book of the Bible, angels visit an old man named Abraham to announce that his elderly wife, Sarah, would have a baby!
- In the second Biblical book, Exodus, the angels are not the ones we like, rather they're the angels of death the Bible says, and they kill the first-born sons of the Egyptians.
- In the Biblical book of Numbers, an angel flashes a sword at a donkey and makes the donkey talk!
- In the Psalms, angels are all over the place doing good things. ***(8/11)*** *We used part of the Psalm in the Call to Worship this morning; the words: "He will command his angels concerning you to guard you in all your ways."*
- In the Old Testament book of Daniel, for the first time an angel is named.

Daniel said, "*I heard a human voice calling, 'Gabriel, help this man understand...' And when he came, I became frightened.*"

No wonder. In Daniel's vision, Angel Gabriel told him about the end of time. That's where we get the idea that the angel Gabriel will blow a trumpet someday to announce the coming of Christ at the end of time.

At the University of Texas, the raucous and loyal Longhorn fans know of Angel Gabriel. They sing of Gabriel in their fight song. Do you know it?

"The eyes of Texas are upon you all the live-long day,

the eyes of Texas are upon you, you cannot get away.

Do not think you can escape them, from night til early in the morn;

the eyes of Texas are upon you...til Gabriel blows his horn."

When the Longhorns beat Texas A&M this fall by a whopping 30 points, they sang that song a lot!

Moving to the story of Jesus, there are more angels. At the empty tomb on the first Easter morning, angels appear to the women to announce the resurrection of Jesus. Later, in the early days of the Christian church, Paul, the writer of several books of the New Testament, refers to angels.

In a biblical reading from Paul's first letter to the Corinthians, often heard at weddings right in this room are the words: *"if I speak in the tongues of mortal and of angels..."*

Later, Paul writes words that are often read at funerals we have right here at Trinity: *"I am convinced that neither death nor life, nor angels, nor principalities...shall separate us from the love of God in Christ Jesus our Lord..."*

Angels - they're everywhere in the Bible.

But, are angels with us still? As we gather this Christmas to hear the Bible story and sing the carols, it seems they are. In a bit we'll sing:

"It came upon a midnight clear, that glorious song of old,

from angels bending near the earth to touch their harps of gold, above the sad and lowly plains, they bend on hovering wing.

And ever o'er its Babel sounds the blessed angels sing."

In this post 9-11, terrorist plagued "sad and lowly" time we live in, we could use a song of hope from angels this year. Yet strangely enough, angels have a lot of competition for our attention these days. There are numerous magical characters of fiction that are big right now.

How many of you have read or seen a *Harry Potter* book or movie? How about Tolkein's, *Lord of the Rings*?

In 2001, the fantasy double-bill of *Potter* and *Rings* ranked first and second at the box office, and it's happening all over again this year. In the first weekend alone, *Harry Potter and the Chamber of Secrets* cleared $88 million. Harry has been big at the bookstore too, having sold a total of 77 million copies in the U.S., so far.

Popular culture is the most sensitive barometer we have for gauging shifts in the national mood. It seems there is an enchanting of America happening, a move to a nostalgic, sentimental, magical vision of a medieval age. But if the vision is imaginary, the longing in our world and our lives for something magical is very real.

Some religious people have been alarmed by this flight into fantasy. They've suggested that good-believing church people burn their Harry Potter books. I'm not about to do that for many reasons, freedom of speech, freedom of the press, the human right to freedom of choice, a passion for recycling, an aversion to smoke pollution and global warming, and, basically, because I like Harry Potter and I was a Tolkein fan back in high school.

We also had equally fantastic fantasy reading when I was a kid - fairy tales including Mother Goose are full of magic, even witches. Yet I'm still a Christian. Some of you grew up with Darth Vader and the Dark Side and you've come out alright.

There is a fine and definite line between fantasy and faith, between the realm of magic and the reality of religion. Stories of fantasy usually turn the weakling into the hero. Stories of faith tell how God empowers people, not so that they can overpower others, but to bring them hope, peace, joy and love.

Stories of faith don't let us escape into a world of fantasy, but rather, show us how faith in God, and God's power, brings real change to our lives.

Fairy tales and fantasy, like Harry Potter, invite us into a new creation.

The story of a young virgin getting pregnant and being visited by an angel may seem like fantasy, but it takes us where we are in **this** creation, and turns it upside-down when heaven comes to earth. God arrives in a baby born of a young woman named Mary and it all seems quite fantastic.

Many Christmas catalogs have been stuffed into my mailbox this fall. In one, was a picture of an upside-down Christmas tree. It's different than the one seen in yesterday's newspaper. It's on a stand...and you see a trunk at the floor but then the smallest branches start working upward to the largest ones to form a reverse triangle. The caption says: "Upside-down Christmas tree."

This remarkable 7-foot inverted tree was originally designed for specialty stores to display their delicate ornaments using a minimum of floor space. Ornaments hang beautifully without being blocked by lower branches. Gifts can be placed around the base of the tree without disappearing beneath it.

What this mail order company has done to the Christmas tree is what angels do at Christmas, and continue to do our world even today. They turn everything upside down. Back to some of those angels flying through the biblical story turning things upside down:

When old, elderly Sarah gets pregnant, and the angels ask, “Is anything too wonderful for the Lord?”

When Mary gets pregnant as a virgin, Angel Gabriel says, “For nothing will be impossible with God.”

Angel Gabriel, when he announces to Mary that she would give birth to the long awaited Savior of the world, blows not his own horn, but God’s horn. Gabriel becomes the angel of hope...hope beyond fantasy...hope that God will enter the world once again and turn our lives upside-down.

Hope beyond fantasy. What is it we hope for these days in this ‘sad and lowly’ world? Of course, we hope and pray for peace all over the earth.

But in our own hearts, some of us are hoping simply for peace at home:

- that our families will get along.
- that our spouses will listen to us and try to understand.
- Some of us hope that a relationship on the brink of brokenness can be restored...that, for once, we will be able to forgive and be forgiven.
- We hope that the grief inside our hearts from those who have died - grandparents and parents, our children - we hope that peace can be a part of this Christmas.
- We hope that our grown kids who have left the nest will miss us as much as we miss them.

- We hope that our money and energy will hold out and up through the final excesses of the season.
- We hope that our health, if it's been uncertain, will be good again...and if it's been good that it'll stay that way.
- If we live alone surrounded only by precious memories of Christmas past, we hope that we can just get through Christmas...yet sometimes when we hear a beautiful carol or see the face of a child, we remember to pray that Christmas will get through us.
- Many of us hope that, for once, we can learn to say "no" to things that don't really matter: the cooking, the last minute shopping and cards, the rush. So that we can see Jesus in the heart of everything, in our hearts, not just for the "holiday," but for always.

Fantasy tells of a time long ago and far away in a fictional place called Middle Earth.

Faith tells of a time long ago and far away, yet as real and recent as today when God comes into the middle of earth, and into the middle of our lives, and turns everything upside-down.

Our hope is that, like Mary, we might be open to the power of the Holy this Christmas, that we might dare give our lives to the Lord fully and forever...that we might hear Angel Gabriel say to us, as he did to Mary, *"Do not be afraid...you have found favor with God."*

Amen.

***

Violated Expectations

December 29, 2002

Luke 2:22-38

When the time came for their purification according to the law of Moses, they brought him up to Jerusalem to present him to the Lord (as it is written in the law of the Lord, 'Every firstborn male shall be designated as holy to the Lord'), and they offered a sacrifice according to what is stated in the law of the Lord, 'a pair of turtle-doves or two young pigeons.'

Now there was a man in Jerusalem whose name was Simeon; this man was righteous and devout, looking forward to the consolation of Israel, and the Holy Spirit rested on him. It had been revealed to him by the Holy Spirit that he would not see death before he had seen the Lord's Messiah. Guided by the Spirit, Simeon came into the temple; and when the parents brought in the child Jesus, to do for him what was customary under the law, Simeon took him in his arms and praised God, saying,

'Master, now you are dismissing your servant in peace,
according to your word;
for my eyes have seen your salvation,
which you have prepared in the presence of all peoples,
a light for revelation to the Gentiles
and for glory to your people Israel.'

And the child's father and mother were amazed at what was being said about him. Then Simeon blessed them and said to his mother Mary, 'This child is destined for the falling and the rising of many in Israel, and to be a sign that will be opposed so that the inner thoughts of many will be revealed—and a sword will pierce your own soul too.'

There was also a prophet, Anna the daughter of Phanuel, of the tribe of Asher. She was of a great age, having lived with her husband for seven years after her marriage, then as a widow to the age of eighty-four. She never left the temple but worshipped there with fasting and prayer night and day. At that moment she came, and began to praise God and to speak about the child to all who were looking for the redemption of Jerusalem.

Dear Friends,

On this fifth day of Christmas, grace and peace to you.

It was a big Christmas Eve here at Trinity. We had a record number of people, nearly 1800, came to worship to hear the Good News and join in praises of the One who is the Prince of Peace and Savior of us all.

Once all the activities concluded here, I made a trip to Rice Lake to spend Christmas Day afternoon with family and friends. It's an annual tradition to enjoy a meal together, gift exchange, and relaxing time with them.

Given the mid-week holiday this year and a funeral on Friday and a wedding yesterday, and Pastor Mary being off to enjoy some year-end vacation time, there wasn't the freedom to stay overnight in Rice Lake this Christmas. Work beckoned, so I left shortly after supper to return home. I've learned that having a little margin between the end of a holiday and the resumption of normal work activities is a good thing for me.

Driving south on US 53 Wednesday evening, I was anticipating time at home to finish reading unopened cards, admire the fine gifts received and simply to relax a bit. That all changed just south of Chetek. Across from the northbound rest area, a gigantic, camouflaged, nocturnal creature appeared in the middle of the highway - just feet in front of my car. A quick thump and a loud crack ensued. There was no chance to veer from this living hazard! Its demise was instantaneous.

My initial thought was, *"At least it wasn't a deer or a dog, only a big fat raccoon."*

I went back to enjoying the Christmas music playing on the radio - until I heard a warning chime. On the dash the icon for the engine coolant came on. Remembering that the southbound rest area wasn't too far down the road, I slowed and began planning a stop there. But before I arrived, other strange, serious, utterly disturbing sounds came forth from under the hood. I pulled over and stopped. The ghost of the raccoon was about to haunt me.

From experience, I know my car's manufacturer has a great roadside assistance warranty. So I got out the number and realized my cell phone has never been handier. A woman down in somewhere like Selma, Mobile or Baton Rouge answered. She assured me that a tow truck would be dispatched; instructed me to wait with my vehicle and if 90 minutes passed with no response, I should call back. It was then I explained to her winter temperatures in Wisconsin. She said she would expedite my request. I thanked her and ended the call.

A blanket in the trunk was my only real emergency winter resource. I'll now believe the weather guy on the TV station who tells us every October about what we should have in our cars during the winter for times such as this.

Curling up in the blanket, and wondering how long the battery would keep the emergency flashers going, I waited. Cars and trucks whizzed by at speeds which made me feel like I was in a small boat on a stormy sea. One young man did stop to check on me.

I explained what happened and told him a tow truck was to come. So he wished me a Merry Christmas, and said he would be in the area in a while, so he'd check back. I was heartened by this stranger's concern.

Back in the cooling cabin of the car, I waited some more, the headlights of cars coming up behind me was almost mesmerizing. While I waited, I wondered about many things. What if this had happened on a remote road; where there is no cell phone coverage? What if it was minus 10 degrees rather than 10 above zero? What if no one stopped to check, and the tow truck didn't come? The waiting seemed longer as my mind envisioned direr straits.

After waiting for about an hour, amber flashing lights appeared. In a matter of minutes, my car was on the flat bed of the truck and the warmth of its cabin was relieving the sting of cold toes and fingers. My wait was over for emergency assistance. The wait for the repairs of a seriously damaged car continues.

I'm not very good at waiting. Are you? The custom of our lives is for faster everything! So we don't learn to wait well. Now, I know it's never easy to wait for things of importance. It is hard:

-waiting for celebrations on Christmas

-waiting for the plane carrying the one we love

-waiting for the morning to relieve the sleepless night

-waiting for the healing word in a bitter argument

-waiting for the labor to be over and the child to be born

-waiting for dying to end and suffering to cease.

It is never easy to wait.

In the Bible reading you last heard today, an elderly man and elderly woman, Simeon and Anna have been waiting. They've been waiting for the Messiah who had been foretold for generations. Simeon was a priest and Anna was an 84-year-old widow who never left the temple, but worshiped day and night. They were waiting for God.

Have you ever waited for God? Have you waited for an answer to a prayer?

Have you ever waited for God to heal your body, mind or heart; relieve you of worry or grief?

Have you ever waited for God to reveal a plan for your life; to guide you and show you the path God wants you to take?

I've had my share of waiting for God and in the more intense waits, I wish I had thought of Simeon and Anna - these wise, seasoned faithful people of the Bible story today. From them, I learn that we have a couple of options when it comes to waiting for God. We can wait passively or we can wait actively for God.

When James Watt was Secretary of the Interior during the Reagan years, he often infuriated environmentalists by his careless treatment of the nation's natural resources. He advocated the granting of oil leases in wilderness areas, and he worked to permit strip-mining in areas adjacent to national parks. Mr. Watt based his decisions on political **and** religious grounds. A fundamentalist Christian, Watt saw no real reason to preserve the environment, since he believed Jesus would be coming soon. With Jesus coming soon there seemed to him no reason to bother taking care of preserving natural resources. While James Watt possessed a faith in God, he waited passively for God, believing there was nothing to be done while waiting.

Waiting actively for God to come is the other option. Active waiting involves doing the things Jesus calls us to do: serve, forgive, care, share. Simeon and Anna did all those things while they waited for God to reveal his son.

Not long before his death, Henri Nouwen, a Catholic priest and noted author, wrote a book called *Sabbatical Journeys.* He told about friends who were trapeze artists, called the Flying Roudellas.

They explained that there is a special relationship between the flyer and the catcher. This relationship is governed by important rules, such as *"The flyer is the one who lets go, and the catcher is the one who catches."*

As the flyer swings on the trapeze high above the crowd, the moment comes when she must let go. She flings her body out in mid-air. Her job is to keep flying and wait for the strong hands of the catcher to take hold of her at just the right moment. One of the Flying Roudellas told Nouwen, "The flyer must never try to catch the catcher." The flyer's job is to wait in absolute trust. The catcher will catch her, but she must wait.

When we wait for God; for whatever purpose, to help, heal or direct, it is possible to get ahead of God. You wait and nothing seems to happen, so you panic and start to work things out on your own. You start trying to catch God instead of waiting for God to catch you. Waiting is an art, and timing is everything.

Simeon and Anna waited for God in absolute trust. They worked and worshiped, performed acts of justice and prayer. They did what they could, and they waited. God did come to them.

It is hard to wait for God. Waiting for God is not like sitting in a darkened, chilly car waiting for the tow truck to come. Waiting for God is more like waiting for an honored guest to arrive at your home. There is much to be done in anticipation of the needs and wishes of the one who is to come.

Every coming of God meets our needs, but sometimes God comes to us in ways which violate the expectations and demands we hold of God:

-We pray for God to give us inner peace, and God comes bringing another struggle.

-We pray for God to come and heal our loved one and instead God comes to us at the edge of a grave and says: *"I am the Resurrection and the Life."*

When old Simeon saw the baby Jesus in the temple that day, he was filled with joy. His wait for God was over.

He said, "*My eyes have seen the salvation of God.*" Simeon's wait for God ended with the ultimate gift.

My friends, at the end of our waiting, God will come and fulfill our deepest and most ultimate need, too.

Amen.

***

Fear and Failure No Longer Thrive

April 20, 2003

Easter Sunday

Mark 16:1-8

When the Sabbath was over, Mary Magdalene, and Mary the mother of James, and Salome bought spices, so that they might go and anoint him. And very early on the first day of the week, when the sun had risen, they went to the tomb. They had been saying to one another, 'Who will roll away the stone for us from the entrance to the tomb?' When they looked up, they saw that the stone, which was very large, had already been rolled back. As they entered the tomb, they saw a young man, dressed in a white robe, sitting on the right side; and they were alarmed. But he said to them, 'Do not be alarmed; you are looking for Jesus of Nazareth, who was crucified. He has been raised; he is not here. Look, there is the place they laid him. But go, tell his disciples and Peter that he is going ahead of you to Galilee; there you will see him, just as he told you.' So they went out and fled from the tomb, for terror and amazement had seized them; and they said nothing to anyone, for they were afraid.

Dear Friends,

Good morning! What a wonderful day and how good it is to be here and to see you all. Christ is risen!

My greetings extend to you all:

-to you who are here as guests and relatives;
-to newcomers;
-to all who simply decided to walk in and join in praise to the God of life;
-and to those who have noticed my absence during my sabbatical and wondered about me in the past three months.

It is good to be back and to be with you again – especially on this most festive day.

Let's pray. God, you are glorious to us on this day of resurrection. We praise you for bringing new life and hope out of death to a world which dies too much and too often and seems to be dying yet. Touch the hearts and minds of each person in this room with your presence. Renew in us your grace, that with the women who came to the tomb that day so long ago, we might find new life. Amen.

The biblical account of Easter is a story well-known to people. The account of the resurrection of Jesus you heard from Mark is one of four accounts in the New Testament of the Bible.

Mark's account is brief and simple. The women come to the tomb. A young man in white announces Jesus is no longer dead but risen. The young man then tells the women to "go and tell others that you'll see Jesus in Galilee."

There is something though, about Mark's story of the resurrection that is troubling and confusing. The story ends with the women leaving, saying nothing to anyone, *for they were afraid.* That's the END, the grand finale of Mark's story of Jesus' life. The whole shebang ends with the women being afraid.

Fear is a universal phenomenon. At some point, we've all been gripped by fear. Some fear is healthy when it alerts us to immediate harm. But many times, fear can be unhelpful, even damaging.

In the time I've been away this winter, huge fears have been embedded in the fabric of the world. I listened to people express fears in many of the countries I visited in the past several weeks, and the fears we experience are often similar.

From China to Romania and down to the Caribbean, people fear the stability of this world. They fear the warring madness between nations. I read in several newspapers that Europeans fear our country and our power. In Ireland, a poll of 800 people responded to this question: Who do you fear more? Saddam Hussein or George Bush? Sixty-nine percent responded that they feared George Bush.

Certainly, terrorism is a fear of people in many countries – not just in the domain of America.

The mysterious respiratory illness that is baffling researchers and health professionals is striking fear in over two dozen countries. Thankfully, I left China in January before I knew of that threat!

Fear, like the women who left the empty tomb that first Easter day, has the ability to divert our eyes and capture our minds so that we miss the reality that surrounds us. And on Easter, the reality is new life. The fears that surround us all the time can kill our souls and wither our faith. Fear, it clouds our eyes so that we cannot see the risen Christ among us.

These are fearful times in the world. I know many of you were concerned for my well-being while I was away traveling, and perhaps wondered about my sanity for going where I did. Your concern is appreciated and your prayers were revealed to me. But as I ventured into distant places in the world amidst the fears, I saw the risen Christ time and again.

I worked as a volunteer in an orphanage in the small village of Tutova, Romania, and Christ was there. In a simple little hospital there are 30 babies and toddlers who are classified as *"failure to thrive"* children.

Some have serious medical conditions. Most were low-birth weight babies. All of them want for touch, mental stimulation and a loving home. They were all beautiful and precious.

The volunteers I partnered with in Tutova and the women who worked there each day brought the new life of the risen Christ to a place where there is little hope. These children came to life whenever one of these women picked them up, hugged them or talked to them. These women are the risen Christ in a place where life has tremendous potential, yet fears for the future of these children is a constant concern. These women are committed to changing the classification of these children from "failure to thrive" to "ready to thrive."

Have you ever failed to thrive? Have you ever failed to thrive in putting your faith out in front of your fears? Have you ever failed to thrive in seeing the risen Christ when dying and death surrounds you?

Have you ever failed, like those women at the tomb, to GO AND TELL that you know a risen Christ who makes a difference in a world of fear and failure?

My Friends, that's what Easter is about! God breaks out of the world's fear and failure and opens the door to abundant and thriving life!

A few weeks ago, I volunteered briefly at a hospital for men dying of AIDS in Port au Prince, Haiti. The simple work there was to apply lotion to these patients, all of whom lived with a death sentence and some of whom were only weeks from death. I wasn't in the room of 30 patients very long before it struck me that most of them would be dead by the end of the summer.

I remember one man in particular. He wanted deep tissue massage! He spoke Creole. I do not. But the language barrier notwithstanding, he clearly told me what, where and how he wanted this massage and it was evident he didn't want me to say "No" to him.

So much of life had already escaped his grasp, I thought, how could I say I couldn't do what he was asking me? So, through an exchange of facial expressions and gestures, he showed me what he wanted.

After I got going, the universal language of the smile acknowledged that I succeeded in meeting his desire. At the same time, I was tending to this patient, a young man dressed in street clothes came in. He spotted me and came right over. My white skin gave me away dozens of times in the past three months!

This young man was carrying a bible, wearing a cross, and he knew some English. He told me he was in training to be a priest. He was there to minister to these dying men.

I asked him, *"What happens to these men when death comes?"*

He explained that people from the Church tend to the body. They have a funeral and burial. But he added, "These men have no family. Their families have abandoned them. We are here to be their family and entrust them to God's care."

While these AIDS patients failed to thrive in this life, as do many children and adults in Haiti where the average life span is 50 years, the good news is still there.

The fear of dying, the fear of a short life span, does not preclude signs of the risen Christ and thriving life. The young priest-in-training then went on to do his work.

A few minutes later, as I was tending to an 18-year-old patient, something amazing happened. It lasted only a short while, but long enough to stir my emotions and place a lump in my throat. I paused in putting the lotion on this young patient with big, deep set eyes that stared off into the distance, so I could watch every face in the room. Here in this ward filled with dying men, cloaked in drab hospital garb and passing their days lying helpless where the air hung hot and heavy - came the risen Christ.

With a small cross placed on a wooden table at the center of the room, the young priest-to-be began praying out loud. Within seconds, this small mass of dying humanity was a heavenly chorus of voices praying together - in a language I didn't understand - but in a spirit that is the risen Christ. At that point, there was no cloud of death blowing through the grey and pallid hospital ward. There was life – life which does not allow fear or failure or even death to have the last word.

You see, there is no way you cannot thrive when the risen Christ comes into view.

My friends, Christ is risen. He is risen indeed. Hallelujah!

Amen.

***

Risk with a Purpose

October 26, 2003

Confirmation Day

Matthew 25:14-29

For it is as if a man, going on a journey, summoned his slaves and entrusted his property to them; to one he gave five talents, to another two, to another one, to each according to his ability. Then he went away. The one who had received the five talents went off at once and traded with them, and made five more talents. In the same way, the one who had the two talents made two more talents. But the one who had received the one talent went off and dug a hole in the ground and hid his master's money.

After a long time the master of those slaves came and settled accounts with them. Then the one who had received the five talents came forward, bringing five more talents, saying, "Master, you handed over to me five talents; see, I have made five more talents." His master said to him, "Well done, good and trustworthy slave; you have been trustworthy in a few things, I will put you in charge of many things; enter into the joy of your master."

And the one with the two talents also came forward, saying, "Master, you handed over to me two talents; see, I have made two more talents." His master said to him, "Well done, good and trustworthy slave; you have been trustworthy in a few things, I will put you in charge of many things; enter into the joy of your master."

Then the one who had received the one talent also came forward, saying, "Master, I knew that you were a harsh man, reaping where you did not sow, and gathering where you did not scatter seed; so I was afraid, and I went and hid your talent in the ground. Here you have what is yours." But his master replied, "You wicked and lazy slave! You knew, did you, that I reap where I did not sow, and gather where I did not scatter? Then you ought to have invested my money with the bankers, and on my return I would have received what was my own with interest.

So take the talent from him, and give it to the one with the ten talents. For to all those who have, more will be given, and they will have an abundance; but from those who have nothing, even what they have will be taken away.

Dear Friends,

A while back I decided it was time to step out into life with greater boldness and abandon. Maybe hitting 40 a few years ago had something to do with it. Or, maybe it was when I prepared my first will and testament, and plainly realized that my life is finite. I don't really recall when I decided to live more boldly, but I do recall why. I simply decided that I wanted my life to be continually growing and experiencing new things – while increasing in faithful service to God and God's people. Since making this decision, I've committed myself to accomplishing one significant challenge, one good-sized risk every year.

Some of the risks, some of the challenges, I've accomplished so far have been perhaps rather frivolous. Others have changed my heart and mind and continue to influence almost every major decision I make.

A couple of the more exhilarating risky challenges to shake me loose a bit have been sports-oriented in nature. I challenged myself to be a bit daring by rafting a Class V whitewater river in Alaska. Another challenge was sky-diving, solo, from 3000 feet in the air.

Now, before you think I've completely lost my mind, let me tell you that more people die each year water skiing or snowmobiling. A psychology professor at a California university researched a large group of high risk competitors including skydivers and race car drivers. He found that 94% of such risk-takers are emotionally stable!

The more thoughtful and enduring risky challenges I've committed to accomplishing have come from international travel in recent years. Three years ago, and again earlier this year, I spent time in the poorest nation in the western hemisphere, the country of Haiti. I lived with a Haitian family both times. Without the convenience of electricity, running water, or basic communication services, I tasted what it's like to live without all the things we take for granted here in Wisconsin.

My bed in the first 12x14' Haitian home was a platform of wood, cushioned by children's clothing, covered with a sheet to form the mattress. We walked about a half a mile to a spring to get water. An open fire was the stove and there was no refrigeration for food. Compared to my comfortable, privileged life here in Eau Claire, living like this even for a few days was a huge challenge. There was plenty of risk stepping into this experience.

All these challenges involved risk – not simply risking breaking a leg or arm, but risking being open to the unknown as well as the uncomfortable.

Risk is reality in this life. Sometimes we choose the risk. Sometimes we don't. Starting a business is a risk. Getting married is a risk. Having children involves risk. Investing your money in the stock market is a risk. Undergoing surgery, driving down I-94, even walking into a church can be a risk.

This morning, 33 high school sophomores are affirming their baptism. When they were baptized 15 years ago, God took a risk in claiming them for the rest of time. When you were baptized, God claimed you and made you a promise. The promise involves God's commitment to you.

In your baptism God says: "You're mine. You belong to me. I'll be with you through the challenges and risks of this life. Even if you walk away from me, I'll still be there loving you, forgiving you and standing by my promise."

After many years of being led in their faith development and understanding of God, these sophomores today will stand up before us to say that they intend to live the rest of their lives following Jesus Christ.

They'll promise to risk living their lives for the purposes of God in this world. In short they're saying to God, "Yes, God, I'm going to live my life for you. I'm going to do what You want me to do because You are first in my life." Wow.

That's a big risk! Following God makes demands on us every single day we breathe the air of this earth. But the demands come only after God has taken the risk to claim us!

I wonder, have you thought about the risk of being Christian? Do you see the risk in following Jesus?

Anybody who follows Jesus must be a risk-taker. Jesus himself said it this way, "If your main concern is preserving your life and your possessions, you won't fit into my company. But if you are willing to a risk and perhaps lose your life or possessions in my service, then you'll fit in just fine." Christians are by nature, risk takers.

In the Bible reading you heard a few minutes ago from Matthew, Jesus makes this truth abundantly clear. Jesus' story is about a master who gave various amounts of money to his servants before he went away on a trip. One was given five talents (in that day a talent meant money and one talent was about $1000). So one servant was given five thousand dollars, another two thousand dollars, and a third servant, one thousand.

Sometime later, the master returned to find that the servant with $5000 had doubled the master's investment. The second servant had also doubled his. But the servant with $1000 had just dug a hole, hid the master's money, and didn't risk anything. So when the master returned, that servant brought the same $1000 and presented it to him. The master was highly displeased and said, "At least you could have put my money in the bank and earned me a little interest." The master knew other investments could have brought a higher return, but with greater risk. The one talent servant wasn't willing to risk anything to grow what the master had given him.

What's the point for us? God expects us to take risks with what God give us. Why? So that we grow in faith and service to God and that God's kingdom will grow, too. God expects us to take risks with what God has given us **for the purpose of advancing the mission of serving others in Christ's love.**

The latest challenge and risk I've committed myself to, is to give more of my life and possessions to advancing this mission of Jesus. Through the mission plan and building expansion God has put before Trinity Lutheran Church, I've committed myself to risk giving more of what God provides me to support this plan. I've always given money to the church, trusting that God multiplies such offerings to serve people. For the next three years, I'm going to a greater extent, a bigger risk than ever before. It's a risk I hope all my Trinity friends will join me in, so that we can stand together to advance the mission of God in this world. It's a risk I hope your family members and friends will take in their home churches, too.

Before I say more about this plan for Trinity, let me tell you a true story about risk. It's a story of how, when we risk putting together our resources, great things can be accomplished.

A few years ago it was my pleasure to meet and visit with Tony Campolo. Tony is an internationally known Christian author and dynamic speaker. I went to Haiti three years ago because Tony Campolo told me to take the risk.

Tony tells of returning to Philadelphia at 8:30 one morning after an overnight flight from the West Coast. His secretary was waiting for him at the airport. She broke the news that he had a women's World Day of Prayer speaking engagement at 10 am. This had somehow missed his calendar. She also told him he was to deliver a "missionary" message.

When Campolo arrived at the church, he was exhausted and not thinking clearly. The only place he wanted to be was in his bed. So when the woman leading this event asked him if he could announce to the gathering that she had received a prayer request from a missionary in Venezuela, Tony didn't respond in normal fashion.

The woman described this missionary as a physician who ran a clinic for the poor. This physician was asking for $5,000 to put an addition on the little clinic so she could handle the crowds of sick people who were coming to see her.

The woman leading this Prayer service then asked, "Dr. Campolo, would you please lead us in prayer that the Lord might provide the $5,000 that is needed by our sister in Venezuela?

Before he could catch himself, Tony said, "No! But what I will do is take all the money I am carrying on me and put it on the altar. And I'm going to ask everyone else here to do the same. No need to write out checks! We'll only accept cash! After we've put all the cash we're carrying on the altar, we'll count it. Then I'll ask God to write out a check for the difference."

It was a good day to pull this off, Tony admitted, because he was only carrying $2.25. The leader smiled benevolently and said, "We've all gotten the point, haven't we?"

"No! I don't think we have!" Tony responded. "My $2.25 is on the altar. Now it's your turn."

The woman was somewhat taken back by his aggressive request, but she opened her wallet and pulled out $110, and slapped it down on top of his meager offering. Then Tony announced to all the ladies, "We're on our way! We've got $112.25. Now it's your turn!"

Tony pointed to a woman who was sitting in the front pew over to his right. She looked around and smiled a bit. Then she got up and came to the altar and put her cash on top of the other two offerings. Tony then got the next woman to do it, then the next, and the next. It took more than twenty-five minutes to take up the offering as one by one, woman after woman came and placed her money on the altar. When they had finished, they counted the money. Together they had given more than eight thousand dollars. Even then, Tony knew that wasn't all the cash in the room. He saw some of the women holding back and putting in meager offerings as they sent dirty looks his way.

At this point there wasn't any time left for Tony to speak. He didn't think they wanted to hear from him anyway, so he simply said to the congregation, *"The audacity of asking God for five thousand dollars, when God has already provided us with more than eight thousand dollars. We should not be asking God to supply our needs. God already has!"*

That puts in perspective the risk of giving away our money and our lives. All the risk is really on God, isn't it? It is, if we truly believe God gives us what we need.

Today, this congregation stands on the edge of taking a big risk of growing the mission of Jesus for our second 50 years together. We are going to invest over $2 million dollars in this facility — a key tool we use in serving people with Christ's love. When the construction is done next year, there will be room for nearly 400 more people in this worship area.

The beauty, functionality and experience of worshiping together in this room will be dramatically improved. We take this risk together as a church, so that we can continue doing what God wants us to do - reach more people with the Good News of Jesus Christ.

I'm excited about this plan. In it, I'm pleased God is moving me personally to take another risk to grow in faith and service to God's people. I hope

God is putting a faith growing risk in your life today, too.

This morning when those 33 sophomores come forward, we'll all be watching the risks they take. The risks which God will put in their path as Christian men and women will surprise, challenge and direct them in ways they can't even yet dream about. But the risks will never overcome them because of that claim God made upon them when they were baptized. It's my hope and prayer for them, and for each one of you, too, that you'll re-affirm the risk of being Christian and step out boldly into the challenges of life – for the purpose of serving people in Christ's love and growing the Kingdom of God.

Amen.

***

Social Graces and Dinner Spaces: A New Order to God's Kingdom

August 29, 2004

Luke 14.1-7,14

On one occasion when Jesus was going to the house of a leader of the Pharisees to eat a meal on the Sabbath, they were watching him closely. Just then, in front of him, there was a man who had dropsy. And Jesus asked the lawyers and Pharisees, 'Is it lawful to cure people on the Sabbath, or not?' But they were silent. So Jesus took him and healed him, and sent him away. Then he said to them, 'If one of you has a child or an ox that has fallen into a well, will you not immediately pull it out on a Sabbath day?' And they could not reply to this.

When he noticed how the guests chose the places of honor, he told them a parable. And you will be blessed, because they cannot repay you, for you will be repaid at the resurrection of the righteous.'

Dear Friends,

This weekend the 2004 summer Olympics in Athens wraps up after a two week run. One of the big news stories of this Olympiad involved Wisconsinite, Paul Hamm. He's the gymnast who captured a lot of attention when a controversy with the judges messed up a Korean gymnast's score. The scoring error resulted in Paul Hamm getting the gold medal - when it should have gone to the Korean.

After the scoring issue erupted, many opinion pieces were written saying Paul Hamm should have returned the gold medal. Some people thought Olympic officials should have given a second gold medal to the Korean gymnast. The most interesting suggestion came from a few writers who suggested that Hamm should have taken his gold medal, walked over to the Korean man and hung the medal around his neck. That would truly have been a magnanimous thing to do.

I really don't want to figure out this controversy. I suspect Paul Hamm's pride was the reason he didn't give away the Gold medal which really belonged to the Korean gymnast.

Pride is something which is a part of all of us. We don't talk about that do we! Jesus did and for those reason we're all going to take a little PQ test right now. PQ = Pride Quotient. All you have to do is just sit right where you are. You don't need a pencil or paper. Listen to the following statements and answer 'Yes' or 'No.' Ready?

1. I enjoy being the object of people's attention.
2. I think I deserve the best.
3. I seldom pass a mirror without looking at myself.
4. I'm not appreciated enough for all that I do.
5. I'm offended if I do something for someone and am not thanked.
6. I seldom ask for help, because I can do the job better myself.
7. I feel pretty good that I didn't answer YES to every question!

If you answered YES even once, you have pride. If you didn't answer YES at all, it simply reveals you are not admitting the truth about yourself. Pride is hard to see in ourselves, but we can easily see it in others, can't we.

The issue of pride kicks off the Bible reading from Luke today. It's a story of Jesus arriving at a dinner banquet one day. Right away Jesus notices how the guests were tripping over each other, seeing who could get the best spot at the table. Shocked at their pride, Jesus tells a story to make his point.

Speaking to the other dinner banquet guests, Jesus gently chides them for their breach of etiquette and pride. In a not-so-subtle way, Jesus says, *"Don't risk showing your pride quotient by taking a seat at the head of the table. Because after all the guests have arrived, you might not be the most honored one and then you'll be told to get up and move to the end of the table. And then what would happen to your pride?*

Jesus' teaching seems to be a lesson in table manners & the social graces, right? It would be, if the story ended right here. But Jesus continues. Next he turns to the host of this dinner party and says:

"When you host a luncheon or dinner party, do not invite your friends or relatives or rich neighbors, in case they may invite you in return, and you would be repaid. But when you host a dinner, invite the poor, the crippled, the lame, and the blind – the people who are overlooked or excluded."

Bad social graces on Jesus' part isn't it? Imagine the dinner host being galled by Jesus and this unsolicited advice. Whoever would throw a banquet and invite the poor, crippled, the outcast people of society?

In telling this second part of the story, Jesus plays God's hand. In this we get a good picture of an inclusive God who has an eye for the people that are marginalized or wrongly judged by society.

In Jesus' day, people who were blind, lame, or poor were outcasts and especially overlooked by religious people. Their afflictions were considered punishment by God for some sin. So they were shut out, excluded. They weren't allowed in religious gatherings like worship.

It would be like Trinity Lutheran Church having signs out in the parking lot saying: *"If you're handicapped, you can't be here."* Or it would be like instructing our ushers to *"keep an eye out for any incoming walkers, wheelchairs, or people on crutches and be sure to turn them away."*

Jesus' advice to this dinner host is just the opposite. When you host a dinner and you invite the poor, lame, blind, outcast, Jesus says you will be blessed — because these folks cannot repay you.

Blessed. You will be blessed when you expand your guest list. When you pay attention and extend love and hospitality to the people the world judges as unfit and unable to give you something in return.

You see, if Jesus had stopped talking after the first part of the story where the guests jockey for the good seats at the dinner table, what would we think? Jesus would sound an awful lot like a first century Miss Manners, right? But Jesus goes on and uses a teachable moment to talk about something near and dear to his heart: the new order of God's kingdom.

In the new order of God's kingdom, everyone has a place at the dinner party. No one is more important than anyone else. There are other Bible stories where Jesus uses banquets to tell us about the kingdom of God. The Bible makes it very clear who is invited to God's banquet. And the guest list is a lot bigger than the religious leaders of Jesus' day imagined. They thought they were so important, deserving of honor. They had a high pride quotient!

But in this bible reading Jesus goes after human pride and says:

Don't get too smug, presuming to know:

*who's a sinner and who's not;

*who deserves God's favor and who doesn't;

*who is invited to the banquet in God's house and who cleans up the table.

Is this a message we need to hear? Does our pride lead us to think that we're better than the person on welfare, the mentally ill, the physically challenged, the poor, uneducated or unemployed?

This Bible reading has Jesus noticing the pride of dinner guests who try to claim power and honor, and a host who needs to broaden the guest list. The deeper message isn't about social graces. It's about God's justice and God's heart for all people — especially the ones who have negligible status.

In the other biblical stories about banquets, Jesus says, *"Everyone is invited. God has a place for everyone."* Everyone! Think about that.

Maybe God isn't big on social graces — to paraphrase the country western singer Garth Brooks. But God is big on inclusivity, justice and calling us to humbly extend the same to all our brothers and sisters.

Amen.

***

Hanging with Sinners

June 5, 2005

Pentecost 3/A

Matthew 9:9-13

As Jesus was walking along, he saw a man called Matthew sitting at the tax booth; and he said to him, 'Follow me.' And he got up and followed Him.

And as He sat at dinner in the house, many tax-collectors and sinners came and were sitting with Him and His disciples. When the Pharisees saw this, they said to his disciples, 'Why does your teacher eat with tax-collectors and sinners?' But when He heard this, He said, 'Those who are well have no need of a physician, but those who are sick, go and learn what this means, "I desire mercy, not sacrifice." For I have come to call not the righteous but sinners.

Dear Sisters and Brothers in Christ,

May the grace and peace of God be yours in abundance.

In the past few years, one mission emphasis of this congregation has been the development of a ministry of health. Incorporating the gifts of many health professionals in this congregation - and others who understand the importance of the link between body, mind and soul, Trinity's health ministry exists to "Serve God's people in Christ's name by ministering holistically to physical, emotional, and spiritual wellness."

Health and healing is a priority of Trinity's wonderful health ministry. Our new Care Team and a fabulously gifted and most fine parish nurse advance a holistic approach to the health of people. Research bears out a connection between faith and health. It is lived out when we are good stewards of our lives.

As much as we advance wellness, there continues to be significant stigma in our society attached to the absence of good health. Thankfully we've grown beyond some stigmas of past eras, yet still today, stigmas attached to illnesses of the human mind persist.

People are very reluctant to admit any kind of emotional or mental affliction for fear that they or their family might be stigmatized. Even though famous people like Barbara Bush, Harrison Ford, Drew Barrymore and Mike Wallace have come out to admit their own battles with depression and anxiety, many people still resist treatment for fear of the stigma.

While we, as a society, have moved from institutionalizing anyone with a mental illness to finding supportive and life-giving ways of main-streaming people, there remains still some stigma.

There are other illnesses that carry a mark of shame. AIDS and HIV are probably at the top of the list. People at risk for AIDS who ought to be tested often aren't for fear that their condition will become public and in turn possibly lose jobs, health insurance, or even family support. Addiction to alcohol, and legal and illegal drugs, is pervasive in our society. Bill Wilson, God bless him, developed Alcoholics Anonymous precisely as a way for people to get help while guarding privacy and anonymity, yet the stigma of addiction remains a tremendous obstacle to people needing help.

From the beginning of time, societies have stigmatized people and behaviors they deemed unacceptable. Often these judgments were cruel, arbitrary, and even irrational. In primitive cultures, people were expelled and sometimes killed on the basis of superstition and blind belief.

In biblical times, people with leprosy were shunned in the belief that their disease was God's curse on them. Even today, superstition, fear, and ignorance play a large role in determining whom we label as shameful and unwelcome. We are especially harsh in judging people whom we consider lacking in self-control. We raise our eyebrows at people who don't keep themselves in control.

Which makes me wonder why there's no stigma attached to being a part of the church. Now, stick with me here. Here's why I say I'm surprised there is no stigma attached to church participation. Most every Sunday we admit that we aren't in control. We regularly confess that we are not in control of our lives - that our attitudes and behaviors are not in keeping with what the Lord wants of us.

In the book of Romans (7:15), we read: *"I do not understand my own actions. For I do not do what I want, but I do the very thing I hate."*

Isn't that true about us? Every time we come here and join in that prayer of confession we are clearly and openly revealing that our sinful lives are in some disarray and that we need help BIG TIME. Yet we're not stigmatized by anyone. We are not outcast because we admit our improper conduct. Nobody comes to worship with a paper bag over their head. I didn't see any of you sneak in here today for fear of being stigmatized. I've never seen anyone come to worship in disguise.

Yet there are people who see Christians - church people - as out of touch or worse yet, hypocrites. We say we are Christians and then we act unbecoming of the God we believe in. In America today, I would venture to guess that the people who have nothing to do with the Christian church think that those of us who do, all fall in one camp. That camp being that Christians are highly conservative, politically right, and notably intolerant.

The recent fight over letting Terry Schiavo die was a feast for pastors and priests, eager to proclaim what they believed was morally and religiously imperative. Millions of people heard and saw the message pronounced in the name of the Christian Church, that if they didn't hold the same position, they were wrong.

My point is that something has gone terribly wrong in the way people understand the Christian Church - and perhaps even in the way Christians see themselves.

Today's bible reading from Matthew reminds us that Jesus had perspectives that challenged people's understanding of God. Jesus hung out with some pretty questionable people. He sat and ate with people who were stigmatized by society. Jesus made a point of seeking out people with bad reputations, and he raised the eyebrows of the respectable people.

In this bible reading, we read about the Pharisees. These were good people. They kept the rules of their faith. They led moral lives and they looked down on people who did not live with those same standards and beliefs. So, in this story of Jesus today, these good religious Pharisees see Jesus eating with tax collectors and sinners. They ask Jesus' disciples: "Why does your teacher eat with tax collectors and sinners?" Jesus obviously overhears and he answers for himself. His response was shocking. "I want you to be merciful to others because I didn't come to invite good people to follow me, I came to invite sinners." (Matthew 9: 13)

Jesus wants to hang with sinners, just as he went to the cross to hang for sinners. Jesus shows his personal interest in, not the good people, not the upright and upstanding, and not the ones with a tight rein on their minds, bodies or lips. Rather, Jesus came for precisely the people most likely to be judged, excluded and seen as shameful. It's not that Jesus wouldn't associate with the respectable folks like those Pharisees. The Bible makes a point of saying that Jesus dined with them, too.

On the other hand, Jesus seems to have had a special place in his heart for the outsiders - anyone shunned or judged. Jesus reached out to those folks in liberal ways, with deep mercy, tender compassion, genuine acceptance - and not a single ounce of contempt.

So, knowing that Jesus wants to hang with sinners, and we are the church of Jesus, then, who should be here in this gathering? Who does Jesus want at his table of Holy Communion? Who does Jesus want in his kingdom? What qualifies a person to be a friend of Jesus?

Given the people Jesus hung out with while he was on earth, I would conclude that the friends of Jesus invited to be a part of his church include:

- anyone who has ever done something illegal or unkind;
- anybody who has ever had a problem with anger or resentment;

I think the friends of Jesus in his church include:

- anyone who's had trouble controlling their sexual thoughts and desires;
- anyone whose bodies won't do what they want them to do;
- anyone who has used another person for personal satisfaction or gain.

I think the friends of Jesus in his church include:

- the sick, handicapped, and addicted;
- the depressed and despairing;
- the straight and gay;
- the underweight and the overweight.

I think the friends of Jesus in his church include:

- people who think they're smarter or stronger or better than others;
- people who think they're dumber or weaker or worse than others.

I think the friends of Jesus in his church include:

- people with problems and people who create problems;
- people who hate other people and people who hate themselves;
- people who worry too much and people who are overly confident,

I think the friends of Jesus in his church include:

- people who put down other people;
- people who don't stand up for themselves.

All these people are of primary concern to Jesus and are to be included in his church.

Add to Christ's church:

- the ungrateful;
- the rich, and poor;
- the impatient;
- the greedy and stingy;
- the gossipy;
- people who take pleasure in other peoples' misfortunes;
- people who waste time feeling sorry for themselves.

Have I left out anybody? You and I are included, too.

Because of Jesus.

Amen.

***

Home for Christmas

Christmas Eve 2005

Prayer:

Lord Jesus, because we could not come to you, you came to us. Because we could not find our way home, you made your home with us. This night our joy is full, our hope is fulfilled, our yearning is met in your great love. For we celebrate again your birth as a human being - one full of grace and truth. Amen.

Dear Friends;

On this Christmas Eve, may the quiet joy, the amazing wonder and the profound goodness of God's grace be with you, and in you, always.

The annual Christmas pageant at Perpetually Pleasant Lutheran Church went well last Sunday. Mary and Joseph came into Bethlehem on cue. There they were met by the nine-year-old innkeeper who dutifully informed them that, though he would love to help them out if he could, there was, again this year, "*No room in the inn. Sorry, "no vacancy, like the sign says out front.*"

But then he looked again at Mary and Joseph, who really did look tired from their journey, and the innkeeper, in a last-ditch attempt at a compassionate solution blurted out, "*But there's a great motel with cable just around the corner from the church!*" At this point the pageant was in shambles.

"*There was no place for them in the inn,*" Mary and Joseph were told. Another way to translate the word "inn" would be to say "guest room."

There was no appropriate place in the guest room was what they were told.

In many of our homes, there is a designated room for overnight guests. We're hospitable people. We would not send out-of-town friends or relatives to a motel - though they might choose to do so on their own.

Mary and Joseph were among relatives. They were back in Bethlehem because Joseph was "*of the house and lineage of David.*" The problem was, there were undoubtedly many relatives back for the government's census.

By the time Mary and Joseph arrived, the guest room was filled. So they had to stay in the next best place in the family home, which would have been the outer room where the family's animals were brought in for safe-keeping during the night. Especially in cool weather, the animals were brought into the outer room for the night. In the morning they would be led away, the room swept, and used for other family activity.

That's where the manger was, the feeding trough for the animals - in this outer room.

Some of you who are home for Christmas or have come to visit relatives will sleep tonight on the couch in the family room, or curled in a sleeping bag elsewhere, because there is no "appropriate place" for you in the guest room. Uncle Oscar from Hurley commandeered that room before you got here. Well, that was probably the case for Mary and Joseph, and Jesus. Rather than send you to the Holiday Inn, because the family loves you so much and is so delighted to have everyone home for

Christmas, they are giving you the honor of sleeping on the floor in the family room.

All of this puts the story of that first Christmas a bit differently. Jesus was not born in the stable of some cold, impersonal hotel, but rather in the outer room of a home where doting aunts, uncles, and other random relatives cooed and fussed over the new baby. In the context of home, Jesus, most vulnerable and needy, was safe amid the blessings of family.

Some of you have made incredible effort to be home for Christmas. You have flown Northwest Airlines. You have suffered the indignities of a crowded, slippery I-94. Tonight, even that fold-out sofa bed, the one with the bar running right across your kidneys, the one with the two-inch foam mattress, will feel good because you are home. Home for Christmas.

Homelessness is much on our mind these days. There are families in this community being housed in a building downtown because they do not have a home - they have nowhere to belong.

We all want to belong. We want someplace where we fit. Remember the opening song of the TV show "Cheers?" "You want a place where everyone knows your name." The song suggests that home is as much a state of mind as a place. It's where you fit. Even if you are alone this night or for this holiday - there is a home for us all. Someone once said, "*Home is not where you live but where they understand you.*" Or of course, Robert Frost, "*Home is the place where, when you go there, they have to take you in.*"

But more than even all that, Christmas, as the Bible tells it, is not just about Mary and Joseph coming home, safe in the guest room. It's not even about your homecoming for Christmas. It's about

God, Lord of Lords, King of Kings, Prince of Peace, Savior, coming home. We couldn't get to God, so God got to us, coming among us in this mundane, ordinary family story we cherish every December. What we call "incarnation" is somebody sleeping on the couch in the family room. That somebody is little Jesus. That's the joy of it.

Why are so many of you here tonight? I think I know why. Moving right into the middle of your family with its love and laughter, secrets and sins, silliness and problems, there comes this God. I think that is why you are here and that's why there is joy.

The final book of the Bible, almost the last chapter of the Bible, ends in a great gush of joy:

"God's home is now with people. God will live with them, and they will be God's own." (Rev 21:3) At home.

Merry Christmas. Welcome home.

Amen.

***

Where the Maps Meet

March 12, 2006

Mark 8:31-38

Then he began to teach them that the Son of Man must undergo great suffering, and be rejected by the elders, the chief priests, and the scribes, and be killed, and after three days, rise again. He said all this quite openly. And Peter took him aside and began to rebuke him. But turning and looking at his disciples, he rebuked Peter and said, 'Get behind me, Satan! For you are setting your mind not on divine things but on human things.' He called the crowd with his disciples, and said to them, 'If any want to become my followers, let them deny themselves and take up their cross and follow me. For those who want to save their life will lose it, and those who lose their life for my sake, and for the sake of the gospel, will save it. For what will it profit them to gain the whole world and forfeit their life? Indeed, what can they give in return for their life? Those who are ashamed of me and of my words in this adulterous and sinful generation, of them the Son of Man will also be ashamed when he comes in the glory of his Father with the holy angels.

Dear Friends,

Some time ago I was at an event where the participants were asked to draw a life map. A life map identifies moments or events which have had a formative effect on your life. In drawing the map, you discover and remember those events that have shaped you and how those events have contributed to where you find yourself today.

A life map consists of plotting moments you've experienced. Things like a graduation, job change, wedding or retirement can cause us to recall points of joy and achievement.

Other events on the life map depict points of struggle and suffering. Things like a health crisis, divorce, death of a parent, child or spouse can cause us to reevaluate priorities, values - even go in an entirely new direction in life.

My longtime friend, Kay, recently buried her mother who had suffered from Alzheimer's disease for a number of years. At the funeral, the grandchild of this family had leadership roles in the service. This was a visible connection to the faith value their grandmother had held so highly.

Now, through the grief of death, Kay is reevaluating her priorities. Quietly, Kay is looking at her own life map and seeing events on that map where her mother had passed on the value of faith. As Kay reviews her life map, she's seeing that the grief of her mom's death is causing her to re-examine her own parenting priorities. She wants to make sure she passes on the value of faith to her own children.

My college friend, Dave, went through a divorce four years ago. Divorce can cause a person to move through an enormous amount of suffering as one recognizes that things didn't work out as planned or desired. That's the case for Dave. He now looks at his life map and sees how that suffering has led to a clearer awareness of the importance of self-examination, forgiveness, and good and loving friends.

Sometime, I hope you'll jot out your life map. Doing so will take you through the public and private joys, laughs, sufferings and wanderings of your life. A life map is a way to see the key events which cause us to feel and experience life from a deeper, more profound vantage point than simply seeing events as achievements or miseries to get through.

I would guess that the life map of every person in this room would include some points of suffering. Yet, isn't it ironic that we live in a culture that doesn't like to struggle with the reality of suffering? We know it exists, and we see it often, but we really do wish it would go away and certainly not come close. The national debate about "compassion fatigue" after an array of disasters last year, amplifies our dis-ease with suffering. We'd rather wrap ourselves in comforts and toys that help us avoid, escape or at least minimize reality.

It is the second Sunday of Lent. The Bible reading is Jesus' first prediction of his suffering and his death. Upon hearing it, the disciple Peter does what most of us would do: "Aw, forget it Jesus, it's not going to happen that way." It's Peter's first denial. Jesus turns Peter around: "Get behind me, Satan, for you are not siding with God, but with humankind."

Suffering is real. Suffering is part of Jesus' life. He wasn't about to deny it, or keep it a secret, or wish that it would go away by not talking about it. Suffering is a life issue and inescapable. It's on our life maps whether we admit it. It is a part of the life journey – no matter how much this current culture wishes it away.

I've traveled to many places in the world and seen suffering in a variety of contexts. In those travels, I've also seen the great symbols of other world religions. The Jewish star, or the smiling, full-bellied Buddha, have a cheerfulness about them. As art - these symbols can lift you.

Yet, as Christians, the great symbol of our faith is the cross. It's not a particularly engaging piece of art, like the happy Buddha. But the brilliance of the cross, it seems to me, is that, in it, as in no other, suffering and love are visibly portrayed together.

In the teachings of Jesus, the cross is neither a prelude to triumph, nor a resurrection symbol. Rather, it is a dreadful burden. In Jesus' days, criminals given a death sentence were required to carry their own cross beam on which they would be hung.

So, in this bible reading today, Jesus claims this controversial symbol as a fundamental principle of discipleship - suffering is part of life. True loss, the giving away of one's self for others, is the gateway of God.

In his first prediction of his future, Jesus tells those gathered around him that "the Son of man must suffer many things." He tells his disciples that unless they are willing to lose their life, they cannot gain life. He tells his disciples to shoulder their own crosses as they follow him into all of life.

Jesus wants us to know that, in living this life of faith, there will be suffering. He wants us to be willing to let go of ourselves and our expectations of this life in order to discover the transformation which is God's will for us in the living of our lives.

We all want good lives. I've never known anyone who said they didn't. I visited recently with a lovely person of this faith community who told me, tears glistening in her eyes, that she merely wanted to be happy and fulfilled in this life. These are worthy wishes for life. We know there is no happiness and fulfillment without some suffering - whether it be our own suffering, or suffering in the people we love.

The transition from our desire for merely human happiness to the deep joy present in the divine encounter with God is bound to involve some moments of sharing in suffering. It is within those times of deep conscious suffering or sharing in another's suffering that we can come alive to the depth and grace available to us in the one who loves us.

Jesus asks, "For what advantage is it, to gain the whole world and lose one's life?"

"We can avoid suffering and the bitterness of suffering," writes Dorthee Solle, "but only for a price that is too high – ceasing to love." As with Jesus, to make the decision to love is to know we will suffer.

Nick Wolterstorff taught college philosophy for his career and he's a dad, too. Nick knows suffering. His son Eric died in a tragic climbing accident at the age of 25.

Nick has done what so many brave teachers have done with the experience of tragedy in their own lives. He has written a small, profoundly powerful book, entitled "Lament for a Son." In the book, Nick dares to raise his voice and his fist to God as he comes to grips with a new understanding of suffering.

He writes: *"What is suffering? When something prized or loved is ripped away or never granted.... What it is, I do not know. As I watch the flicker of ... evening light on still water, this thought overwhelmed me: I understand nothing of suffering. Of pain, yes; cut fingers, broken bones. Of sorrow and suffering, nothing at all. Suffering is a mystery as deep as any in our existence. Suffering may keep its face hid from each, while making itself known to all.**

"We are one in suffering. Some of us are wealthy, some bright; some athletic, some admired. But we all suffer. For we all prize and love; and in this present existence of ours, prizing and loving yield suffering. Love in our world is suffering love. Some do not suffer much because they do not love much. Suffering is for the loving." ("Lament for a Son," page 83.)

This is the legacy of the cross for us. It is the story of God. It's the story of God in Jesus being able to love the world and those in it so much that he was willing to suffer for that love. The cross becomes then, a symbol of willful loss of self in order to acquire the new life God will give to us through the experience of 'suffering love.'

When I look at my life map, I see that the moments of deep change and transformation came when I quit chasing happiness and took up the cross and followed, not knowing whether happiness or fulfillment would be part of the equation. And the key moments have come when I had little idea what I was doing or where I was going.

It is the moments of great suffering in this life that make us human and aware of God. Sometimes it's the personal moments of suffering - such as the death of someone we love, the loss of something precious.

Sometimes, the suffering is over the great groaning tragedies of the world, the horror of Holocaust, the suffering of whole nations and races of people in Iraq, sub-Saharan Africa and Palestine. It is the suffering moments of this life that make us alive, make us human, and make us more deeply and consciously loving. It is the gateway to our being able to begin to comprehend what is the depth of love and grace of God for us.

"There's a wideness in God's mercy, like the wideness of the sea," claims the hymn. It is so.

The story of Jesus is that He, "must suffer many things, and be rejected by the elders and be killed and after three days rise again." Jesus wouldn't let Peter deny this suffering. At Lent, we tell this story as a reminder that within Jesus' story is our story. On this amazing journey we call life, there will be encounters with human suffering. There will be, in our living, sorrow, despair, rejection, grief, even horror – all suffering.

We know, too, from Jesus' story, and our own stories, through the suffering there will be a deepened capacity to love. For this is the transformational power contained in our suffering, we learn love.

Amen.

*Wolterstorff, Nicholas, Lament for a Son, W.B. Eerdmanns, 1987. p 83

***

After the Music Stops

April 9, 2006

Palm/Passion Sunday

Mark 15:2-15

Pilate asked Him, 'Are you the King of the Jews?' He answered him, 'You say so.' Then the chief priests accused him of many things. Pilate asked him again, 'Have you no answer? See how many charges they bring against you.' But Jesus made no further reply, so that Pilate was amazed.

Now at the festival he used to release a prisoner for them, anyone for whom they asked. Now a man called Barabbas was in prison with the rebels who had committed murder during the insurrection. So the crowd came and began to ask Pilate to do for them according to his custom. Then he answered them, 'Do you want me to release for you the King of the Jews?' For he realized that it was out of jealousy that the chief priests had handed him over. But the chief priests stirred up the crowd to have him release Barabbas for them instead. Pilate spoke to them again, 'Then what do you wish me to do with the man you call the King of the Jews?' They shouted back, 'Crucify him!' Pilate asked them, 'Why, what evil has he done?' But they shouted all the more, 'Crucify him!' So Pilate, wishing to satisfy the crowd, released Barabbas for them; and after flogging Jesus, he handed him over to be crucified.

Dear Friends,

When I was in college, I volunteered as a Big Brother, in the Big Brother - Little Brother program of the Fargo-Moorhead community. My little brother was a fifth grader name Tyson. Tyson was a quiet, tentative kid - who with his mother and two younger sisters lived in Fargo after the death of Tyson's dad.

The Big Brother organization in Fargo was supportive and helpful in providing opportunities for adults and kids to engage in fun and educational activities. One of the events they set up involved hosting birthday parties at area nursing homes. In one visit to a nursing home with Tyson, I realized this was right up his alley. He loved the residents - especially the elderly women who reminded him of his great-grandmother.

So it became our habit to visit the nursing home regularly. Tyson and I became attached to an 88-year-old resident named Mabel. Mabel liked to walk around a lot - always on the move wandering up and down the hallways or riding the elevator. When she did sit still, no one ever seemed to sit by Mabel. She never had any family visit her that I can remember. Unfortunately, Alzheimer's Disease had gotten the best of Mabel. She spent most of her time in idle chatter, usually senseless to those of us around her.

One time when Tyson and I were visiting the nursing home, just as the elevator doors were closing, in popped Mabel to join us on our ride. Right away she greeted Tyson and tweaked his cheek. As she looked at him, touching his soft skin and silky blonde hair, she hummed a lullaby as something seemed to come over her. As we neared the end of our ride, Mabel and I had the only intelligible conversation that I can remember in the years I knew her. She put her hand on my elbow and with a twinkle in her eye, she whispered in my ear she had a secret to tell me. I think it must have been the twinkle in her eye that caught me off guard as I heard myself responding, "What's your secret Mabel."

"I'm going to have a baby!" she whispered and giggled.

At the wise old age of nineteen, the incident struck me as quite funny. As I have grown older, and been around more children and older folks, Mabel's secret has become more and more profoundly special to me. Despite the cloudy, foggy world of Alzheimer's which surrounded her, even though her mind continued to deteriorate as the end of her life grew ever nearer, Mabel was still able to connect with and delight in birth and new life. Totally forgotten were the morning sickness and labor pains, the long nights of no sleep being up with a new baby, all the dirty diapers, the total dependency - all forgotten. To have a new life of a young child around her gave Mabel, as with most new parents and grandparents, a reason to celebrate and express joy. I can still see it in her eyes.

When I think of the births of our children and grandchildren, my years of visiting at the nursing home and simply reflecting on the highs and lows of living, I am reminded of how intimately connected birth, life and death (beginnings and endings) truly are. Whenever we find we are reaching the end to some part of our lives, it is usually accompanied by the beginning of something new as well.

Jesus knew this to be true. The drama of this week reminds us of that. By following him to death and resurrection, we are encouraged to surrender our lives and trust, even in the face of great suffering and hostility. Jesus shows us that the next step made in trust and faith is met by a grace all sufficient to whatever the challenge before us. As Christian people, we, too, must know the connection between dying and rising, endings and beginnings.

Think about the beginnings and endings in your own life. Going off to school, your first love, graduation, going off to live on your own for the first time. Perhaps it's a wedding day, having to say goodbye to a loved one, changing jobs, moving, retiring. These times are often confusing. We have so many contradictory feelings: sorrow and joy, certainty and fear, hope as well as doubt.

The people of Jerusalem, and especially Jesus, must have experienced something like that on this day we remember as Palm Sunday.

Jesus bounced along the streets on a commandeered donkey. The crowds shouted praises as they pulled branches from trees and threw their garments on the road before him. Surely Jesus knew that he was being watched by the authorities who were threatened by him. Jesus knew there were concerns that his popularity and presence could easily incite a riot.

As he approached the city gates, a shadow loomed over him and a chill pierced his heart like a knife. It is the shadow of a place called Golgotha - a place of endings. Jesus knew that road was leading him to an ending. Yet he rode on in the midst of all the cheering, hoopla and singing, "Hosanna to the Son of David!" "Blessed is he who comes in the name of the Lord!"

What happened after the music stopped?

One of my theories about how people manage with life likens life to a dance. Some people get so caught up in the dance that they fail to ever ask themselves the question of what happens when the music stops. Other people are so caught up in worrying about what happens when the music stops, that they fail to ever get into the rhythm of the dance at all! Most of the people fall on the spectrum somewhere in-between, having considered the question of what comes after the music stops, but still enjoying the dance itself, too.

Palm Sunday is a day to join the dance, to get caught up in shouting loud Hosannas to our King, for waving our palm branches high. We must not fail to ask ourselves the question "What happens after the music stops?"

Jesus, our King comes. He comes not with power and glory, but as a lamb to the slaughter. There isn't a way to escape the reality that there can be no new life without suffering and death beforehand. So we know that the road now lined with garments and palms where music and cheering prevail will, and must, lead us to the agony and silence of the cross - and all the suffering we see around us.

What happens when the music stops and the Hosannas die down, is that the weeping begins, for we see that the fingers wrapped around the palm branches will become fists clenched with pounding hammers, faces splattered with blood as nails pierce him through. Then we sit in silence, waiting to hear the Word.

God be with us after the music stops.

Amen.

***

More Than Roses and Chocolates

January 28, 2007

I Corinthians 13:1-13

If I speak in the tongues of mortals and of angels, but do not have love, I am a noisy gong or a clanging cymbal. And if I have prophetic powers, and understand all mysteries and all knowledge, and if I have all faith, so as to remove mountains, but do not have love, I am nothing. If I give away all my possessions, and if I hand over my body so that I may boast, but do not have love, I gain nothing.

Love is patient; love is kind; love is not envious or boastful or arrogant or rude. It does not insist on its own way; it is not irritable or resentful; it does not rejoice in wrongdoing, but rejoices in the truth. It bears all things, believes all things, hopes all things, endures all things.

Love never ends. But as for prophecies, they will come to an end; as for tongues, they will cease; as for knowledge, it will come to an end. For we know only in part, and we prophesy only in part; but when the complete comes, the partial will come to an end. When I was a child, I spoke like a child, I thought like a child, I reasoned like a child; when I became an adult, I put an end to childish ways. For now we see in a mirror, dimly, but then we will see face to face. Now I know only in part; then I will know fully, even as I have been fully known. And now faith, hope, and love abide, these three; and the greatest of these is love.

Dear Sisters and Brothers in Christ,

In last fall's elections Wisconsin voters were faced with a referendum to change the state's constitutional definition of marriage. For years that definition has stated that marriage is between husband and wife.

In 2005, the Wisconsin state legislature reacted to the national debate over extending the legal benefits of marriage to same sex couples. In that year, our elected representatives moved to change the state's constitutional definition of marriage to read "between one man and one woman." The next step was the referendum which went before voters last November.

Throughout the campaign, political action groups on each side of the referendum jockeyed to find ways to title this proposed amendment. A group opposed to the referendum touted fairness. Their jingle stated, "A Fair Wisconsin Votes 'No.'" A group in favor of the change waved signs reading, "Vote Yes for Marriage - One Man, One Woman."

However one voted on the referendum, and notwithstanding the outcome (it passed), the whole issue of marriage was put in the spotlight for us. Supporting and sustaining the sanctity of marriage is a worthy goal of any society. Wrestling with issues of justice for same sex couples is far from over I suspect. In the light of the entire debate over the definition of marriage and who should be allowed the legal arrangement of marriage, I think we all know marriage has taken a terrible beating in the past 40 years.

Each year, 1 million people divorce in this country *("Rebuilding" pg. 28 by Bruce Fisher and Robert Alberti, 2006 Impact Publishers).* In the late 1970's the rate of divorce peaked and has gently decreased since, though it is still double the rate in the 1940's and 50's. Researchers caution that the declining number of divorces in recent years may be due more to the fact that many couples are choosing long-term cohabitation rather than marriage. In my own experience as a pastor in this congregation, I can tell you that ten years ago maybe half of couples arranging weddings in this church were living together. Today that number is nearly 100%. All these statistics indicate that a dramatic societal shift is underway.

Laura Kipnis, a professor of media at Northwestern University and writer for the New York Times *("Should This Marriage Be Saved" The New York Times, January 25, 2004)* reports that today about half (56%) of all adults in this country are married, compared with three-quarters of adults (75%) just thirty years ago. When it comes to households with children living with married parents, the number today is half of what it was in the early 70's.

Not only has the face of the American family changed, so has the emotion, too. A recent (2005) Rutgers University study of married couples indicates that, "40% do not describe themselves as very happy" in their marriages.

Why are so many marriages failing? Why are so many more submerged in low-level misery or emotional stagnation? You don't have to be a sociologist to know that marriage over the last generation suffered the brunt of huge social and economic changes. The changing role of women, the influence of media and technology, hectic work and recreation schedules of adults and children, shifting economic realities and a host of other factors all contribute to this social change.

We all know that, today, if you want a middle class lifestyle, typically two incomes are needed.

Even the definition of middle class has changed. Our appetite for larger houses, vacation homes, multiple cars, big ticket toys and expensive tastes have upped the budget necessary to be middle class. The toll this enacts upon our relationships is keen. We now have to work and earn more to satisfy ourselves. The demands which go along with this lifestyle now consume more of our time and energy.

Basic logic says that leaves less time and energy to invest in working on healthy, loving relationships with spouse, children, friends and extended family. You've heard the slogan, "Good relationships take work." After long days at work, do any of us find this an attractive proposition? Do we want to come home and work some more? If we are unwilling to do the work needed for good relationships and healthy community, what are the options?

One option, I suppose, is to lose ourselves in the material comforts we've worked hard to earn (the cabin, the HDTV, the toys). Another option is to leave the stagnant, lifeless relationships behind in hopes that something better will come along so that you'll feel happy once again.

In this time of great change and transition in American life as we know it: in marriages, families, friendships, and communities, I see a well-spring of hope. It is clear that we can reclaim a more excellent way of being in relationship with each other for the benefit of families, friendships, marriages and the greater community.

In the bible reading from I Corinthians, the writer, a man named Paul, gives us the hope. While he is not addressing the issue of marriage per se (though this passage of scripture is commonly read at weddings), Paul is addressing the foundational piece of all healthy relationships.

He's writing to the Christian community in a place called Corinth. This city which existed centuries ago, was a hub of economic and cultural life. The people of that time and place were experiencing great distress as they were beating each other up. While they didn't wrestle with the demise or definition of marriage, they were tearing themselves and their relationships apart over who was more right, more gifted, more important. It's not all that unlike the debate we endured in last fall's election.

So the biblical writer, Paul, in hopes of building community and improving relationships for these people, lifts the debate to a single plane - and offers direction for a way of becoming a better community – healthier in relationship. In doing so, Paul lifts up the way of love as what is truly indispensable for all relationships.

Now, I know I'm getting into a most difficult subject to get a handle on. Defining love is challenging! We talk about love in such funny ways. We speak of "falling in love" as if it were a hole. We use the same word when talking about people in our lives as well as desserts! We say "I love my husband. I love ice cream. I love my I-pod. I love a massage. I love my SUV. I love God." How do we take hold of this word?

Well, we best go back to the bible to get a handle on how to speak about love. Thanks to the writer Paul, we see a very clear definition of love that has a firmness about it that denies all sentimentality. The love noted in the bible reading is more than words or even noble actions. This love goes straight to the heart of the problems of human communication and the fractious habits that drive us apart.

What I see here is a no-nonsense definition of love. For those of us who are romantics, love may mean roses, chocolates and candlelight dinners. But for Paul, love doesn't find itself up in the clouds, behind rose-colored glasses or skipping into the sunset together. Noting behaviors and urges that we all have within ourselves, Paul says love is not: impatient, unkind, envious, jealous, rude, selfish, irritable, resentful, deceitful or dishonest.

Let's admit it - we all can see in ourselves each of these behaviors.

So the bible reading goes on to tell us what love is: patient, hopeful, enduring, and believing. Why is this so hard for us in so many of our relationships? Could the demanding loads of responsibility we heap on ourselves, the dizzying pace at which we and our families move and the exhaustion that always lies just below the surface of our skin be diverting us from the work of loving each other?

There's one final thing that is most amazing to me in this whole chapter on love. There is no explicit mention of Jesus. Paul, who knows Jesus as the Son of the Living God, does not once bring up the name of Jesus; but then, maybe he didn't have to. Who else can love us so patiently, so kindly, so generously? Who else loves us through thick and thin, through divorces and separations, not counting the cost? Who, but Jesus, loves us so freely that we can "put an end to childish ways" and aspire to grow to love one another as Christ does in fact love each and every one of us?

These are, I suppose tough times for marriages. Many of the eternal supports that once held people together have fallen away. My friends Carolyn and Mike joke that after their first year of marriage they might have gotten a divorce. Except they didn't because they were so poor and they feared the reaction of their parents. A marriage held together by fear and economic necessity is not exactly built on solid ground.

There has to be more. There has to be love, but not the roses and chocolates kind of love that sends so many of us running to the altar. For there to be community, for there to be family, for there to be relationships of care and compassion that endure the onslaught of time and the terrors of change, there has to be the love that will not let go, that will not fail, that will not write me or you off no matter how miserably short we fall of love.

And for me, that means there has to be Jesus.

Amen.

***

The Truth About Trees

August 9, 2009

Ephesians 4:14 - 5:2

We must no longer be children, tossed to and fro and blown about by every wind of doctrine, by people's trickery, by their craftiness in deceitful scheming. But speaking the truth in love, we must grow up in every way into him who is the head, into Christ, from whom the whole body, joined and knitted together by every ligament with which it is equipped, as each part is working properly, promotes the body's growth in building itself up in love.

Now this I affirm and insist on in the Lord: you must no longer live as the Gentiles live, in the futility of their minds. They are darkened in their understanding, alienated from the life of God because of their ignorance and hardness of heart. They have lost all sensitivity and have abandoned themselves to licentiousness, greedy to practice every kind of impurity. That is not the way you learned Christ! For surely you have heard about him and were taught in him, as truth is in Jesus. You were taught to put away your former way of life, your old self, corrupt and deluded by its lusts, and to be renewed in the spirit of your minds, and to clothe yourselves with the new self, created according to the likeness of God in true righteousness and holiness.

So then, putting away falsehood, let all of us speak the truth to our neighbors, for we are members of one another. Be angry but do not sin;

do not let the sun go down on your anger, and do not make room for the devil. Thieves must give up stealing; rather let them labor and work honestly with their own hands, so as to have something to share with the needy. Let no evil talk come out of your mouths, but only what is useful for building up, as there is need, so that your words may give grace to those who hear. And do not grieve the Holy Spirit of God, with which you were marked with a seal for the day of redemption. Put away from you all bitterness and wrath and anger and wrangling and slander, together with all malice, and be kind to one another, tender-hearted, forgiving one another, as God in Christ has forgiven you. Therefore be imitators of God, as beloved children, and live in love, as Christ loved us and gave himself up for us, a fragrant offering and sacrifice to God.

Dear Sisters and Brothers in Christ,

There once lived a couple in a small house in the city. One day the man noticed that a tree was starting to grow through the living room floor. He thought about mentioning it to his wife. He didn't, lest he appear foolish. For who had ever heard of a tree growing through the living room floor? His wife noticed the tree also, but didn't say anything either. With each passing day, the tree grew larger. The couple watched the tree grow but they never mentioned it, for who had ever heard of a tree growing through the living room floor?

Time passed. Every fall the tree would shed its leaves on the rug and it was really quite a mess. The couple had to spend a good deal of time cleaning up around the tree. But they never mentioned it to each other. For no one had ever heard of a tree growing through the living room floor.

As time went by, the trunk grew thicker so the couple had to make a bigger detour around it to get to the other side of the room. As the branches grew and spread out, they had to bend their heads in walking about the room. But neither mentioned the tree to each other. For who had ever heard of a tree growing through the living room floor?

As the months went on, the couple spent more and more of their time cleaning the rug, ducking under the branches, and sucking in their stomachs to get around the tree in the living room. Both were thoroughly unhappy with the situation. But neither saw fit to mention it. For who had ever heard of a tree growing through the living room floor?

One day, however, the man said to his wife, "It seems that there's a tree growing through the living room floor." His wife said that she, too, had noticed it and wasn't very happy about it, because she had to clean up after it. The man said that he was tired of sucking in his stomach to get around the tree. So the next day, they had the tree removed. The couple was much happier.

After that, whenever a tree started growing through the living room floor, they removed it before it got to be too much of a problem.

I do not know this couple. I do not know the address for their house. But I suspect there are a good many of trees to be found in the living rooms across America - even right in our fair city.

Sometimes people let me see their trees. They even ask my help in cutting them down. But before a tree can be removed, there must be some prior acknowledgment that the tree exists.

Which brings us to our first truth about trees growing in living rooms. The tree is not the problem. Alright, by now you're probably asking yourself, "What is the tree he's talking about?"

So, like Jesus who often answered a question by asking another, the reply would be, "What is it that you are not talking about that is beginning to cause difficulties in some aspect of your life?"

Lots of trees that grow through living room floors relate to matters of the body. Ask physicians and they'll tell you the same thing. There is the physical exam we do not have, the diet we do not follow, the symptom we do not treat, the signal we do not heed. Some of the trees relate to the alcohol we consume or the pills we swallow. Again, the problem is not the tree. The problem is in the lack of acknowledgment.

Jesus knew that the trees that grow through our living room floors often pertain to our relationships with one another. The Bible reading this day helps us to acknowledge that we need guidance to better those relationships - cut down the trees and live more Christ like lives.

The Bible gives us ample evidence of how Jesus dealt with trees growing through living room floors. In the first Bible reading today, you saw Jesus approached by a woman who heard him saying, "I can give you water so that you will never be thirsty again." (John 14:4).

She said, "Jesus give me this water."

He replied, "Go, call your husband, and come back."

The woman answered Jesus, "I have no husband."

Jesus said to her, "Alright, we both know you have already had five husbands. Cut down the tree in your living room, lady!"

As Jesus acknowledged her past, He didn't judge or shame her. In fact, the woman went back home, marveling that anyone could know so much about her and still care for her. And perhaps trees never grew in her living room again.

Another example of Jesus pointing out the tree growing in the living room was seen in an encounter with a rich young man who was looking for more purpose in his life. His money and possessions were just not providing a lot of meaning for him so Jesus said:

I like you young man. I understand that you have a great deal of money. But it's also clear to me that your love for money is greater than your love for anything else...including me. So give it up, already - then come and follow me!

Matthew 19:16-21

The Bible reading from Ephesians today aims to encourage us to be more like Jesus in our living. But to do so, we cannot have trees growing in our living rooms. Why? Because they get in the way of living like Jesus.

The guy who wrote Ephesians knew that trees in the living room deter us from facing our sins and shortfalls. He makes clear there is no room for denials which keep us locked in the OLD LIFE before Jesus saved us from our sin. Instead, the Bible says, "put on the new self, created to be like God."

You see, our denials prevent us from stepping into the NEW LIFE that Jesus provides to us.

Yet, we all know about the trees in the living room, don't we? An array of problems we live with can be linked to denial. Some people do not talk about money and how it is made or spent. Other people avoid expressing doubts about their faith. Sometimes the most difficult tree to acknowledge is about love that is not being exchanged in the marriage for fear that love is perhaps being shared somewhere else. But the point is still the same. The tree is not the problem.

Which leads to a second truth about trees in the living room. Most trees thrive on neglect. One of the most amazing things about the challenges we have in life, especially pertaining to relationships with each other, is how seldom things go away as a result of being ignored. This is a hard truth to acknowledge. Lots of us would like to believe that just the opposite is true.

By nature, we'd rather skirt problems than face them. We would like to believe that you really can let sleeping dogs lie and, either they will never wake up or, if they do, they will arise with sweet dispositions and faulty memories. We fool ourselves thinking that time really does heal all things, even though we know that very few things are healed by time and that most things are healed by people. Trees thrive on neglect.

This leads to a third truth about trees in the living room. We delude ourselves if we think that not acknowledging their existence means that they will have no power to affect our lives. Recall that the tree in the story extracted enormous concessions from two people who could never acknowledge its presence. They had to clean up after it, detour around it and duck under its branches. The Bible reading today tells us, "*You were taught to put away your former way of life, your old self, corrupt and deluded.*"

Some years back, one of my dad's cousins out on the west coast wrote our family history. He assembled family tree information and stories about how my great-grandparents made their way from Norway to these parts in the 1880s.

In telling some stories of my great-grandparents, he wrote about a child born to them before they got married. Back in the late 1800's, unlike today, there was huge shame attached to conceiving a child out of wedlock.

When the family history was complete, copies were shipped to Wisconsin to one of my uncles. He functioned as the distribution agent and also the self-appointed editor of our family history. For before we each received our copies, Uncle Ray made sure to take a big black marker and cover up this reference to the illegitimate child. So strike it from the family history! Let the tree in the living room live on!

Some of us still live in family systems where dirty linen or the tree in the living room is never to be acknowledged! But do not delude yourself into thinking that unacknowledged trees take no toll. They do. They take an enormous toll. It takes great personal energy to maintain a system of denial for very long.

This passage from Ephesians is filled with teachings that give us the encouragement to acknowledge that we fall short, we sin, we make messes of our relationships with each other. This Bible reading doesn't just leave us in that old life. It guides us in walking away from the old, sinful way of life, and into the new self, like God.

Paul, as he writes the practical words for faithful living, wants us to cut down the trees in the living room. Then he gives us directions so that we can live a new and hopeful life because Jesus, in his life, death and resurrection has opened the way from the old life to the new. The directions for this new way of life are:

- put away the denials and lies;
- speak the truth to others, and let not evil talk come out of your mouth;

- be angry but do not sin, put away bitterness and slander;
- be kind to one another, tenderhearted, forgiving one another, as God in Christ has forgiven you

Finally, this Bible reading ends with some reassurance even as it gives us a mission: Be imitators of God **as beloved children.** We don't imitate God in order to become children of God. Because Jesus loved us and gave himself for us, we are God's children already. We don't imitate God to become better people, though when we do this will surely happen. We imitate God for each other and our neighbors across the world.

So, by acknowledging the trees in the living room, cutting them down, moving out into a new, Christ-like way of life, we become better people who share with those in need, build up relationships, and speak loving words to give grace to those around us.

In this way, we truly imitate Jesus and the world is blessed through us.

Amen.

***

Two Parades Then; Two Parades Now

April 17, 2011

Palm Sunday

Matthew 26:1427

Then one of the twelve, who was called Judas Iscariot, went to the chief priests and said, 'What will you give me if I betray him to you?' They paid him thirty pieces of silver. And from that moment he began to look for an opportunity to betray him.

On the first day of Unleavened Bread, the disciples came to Jesus, saying, 'Where do you want us to make the preparations for you to eat the Passover?' He said, 'Go into the city to a certain man, and say to him, 'The Teacher says, My time is near; I will keep the Passover at your house with my disciples.' So the disciples did as Jesus had directed them, and they prepared the Passover meal.

When it was evening, he took his place with the twelve; and while they were eating, he said, 'Truly I tell you, one of you will betray me.' And they became greatly distressed and began to say to him one after another, 'Surely not I, Lord?' He answered, 'The one who has dipped his hand into the bowl with me will betray me. The Son of Man goes as it is written of him, but woe to that one by whom the Son of Man is betrayed! It would have been better for that one not to have been born.' Judas, who betrayed him, said, 'Surely not I, Rabbi?' He replied, 'You have said so.'

While they were eating, Jesus took a loaf of bread, and after blessing it he broke it, gave it to the disciples, and said, 'Take, eat; this is my body.' Then he took a cup, and after giving thanks he gave it to them, saying, 'Drink from it, all of you.

Dear Sisters and Brothers in Christ;

On this Palm Sunday, grace and peace be with you all.

There's a book entitled "When The Cheering Stopped" that tells the story of the fanfare and accolades that surround President Wilson following WWI. When that war ended, Wilson was an international hero. There was a great spirit of optimism abroad. People actually believed that the last war had been fought, and the world had been made safe for democracy.

On his first visit to Paris after the war, Wilson was greeted by cheering mobs. He was actually more popular than their own heroes. The same thing was true in England and Italy.

The cheering lasted about a year. As memory of the war victory faded, so did the cheering for President Wilson. Political leaders in Europe became more concerned with their own agendas.

At home, Woodrow Wilson ran into opposition in the U.S. Senate, and his League of Nations was not ratified.

Under the strain of it all, the President's health began to break. He suffered a stroke, and in the next election, his party was defeated. So it was, that Woodrow Wilson, a man who barely a year earlier had been heralded as the new world Messiah, came to the end of his days, a broken and defeated man.

It's a sad story, but one that is not altogether unfamiliar. It happened that way to Jesus. As we pick up the Bible story, we read about the cheering mobs that greeted him as he entered Jerusalem from the east for the Passover.

There was a second parade that entered Jerusalem that day. It was an armored procession, a military parade. From the west, the Roman governor named Pilate entered from his home on the west coast of Israel.

Pilate's entry was a show of might, power and authority. It was standard practice for the Roman governor to enter the city for major Jewish festivals. Passover was a major festival, one in which the people remembered their liberation from an earlier empire.

Pilate's parade into the city was to make a statement, and he made sure it was lost on no one. The emperor was not only the emperor of Rome, but also one considered to have divine power and authority over all people, nations and cities. Jerusalem was a city of some consequence, and Rome needed to reassert its domination.

Only the Emperor was God.

Imagine Pilate's parade - there are horses and saddles, bridles and whips. Soldiers swarm around their leader with helmets, swords and shields. This parade is an awesome show of power and might, demanding that the people pay attention along the road.

The other parade, with Jesus, enters from the opposite side of town. This one is more like a well-planned street theater. Jesus comes from the countryside, from Galilee, east of the city.

Imagine Jesus on a young colt, too small for a grown man. He rides down a hill into the city and folks begin pulling palms from the trees to welcome him. The excitement cannot be contained. They begin to throw their coats down on the ground in greeting and gratitude.

As he enters, they begin to chant, "Blessed are you! Blessed are you who comes in the name of the Lord. Hosanna to the Son of David!"

Two parades; two very different parades.

Every so often, the news shows us street theater. Street theater draws attention to a particular issue and acts it out in a public location. While in college, there was a street theater troupe that offered dramas around campus to educate people about the issues of the day. Imagine Jerusalem that day - a contrast of street theater entering on opposite sides of town.

Jesus enters Jerusalem with humility, riding a donkey. He walks as a peasant with the poor. He rides alone, but is surrounded by excitement, welcome and love.

Spirit is in the air! So is hope for the coming of a just and visionary leader. What a sight it must have been!

Two parades. Two statements of leadership. Two ways of walking in the world. Two ways of presenting power and the authority of God.

Which parade would have captured your attention that day? Which display of power best fits your understanding of God's power at work in our world today?

The parade with Pilate looks as if it leads into a good life. It's got the strong, resolute leader. He commands authority. This parade promotes the look of an organized society. It places a stamp of approval upon the empire of the world and acknowledges the power of the state and even regards the state as a religious authority. Cesar is King of Kings and Lord of Lords.

The other is a parade, which will lead to a death later in the week, has Jesus at the center.

It's a parade that garners the hopes of the poor and the lost, those who don't have access to the powers of society. This parade lifts the hopes of people who have been ignored, and marginalized by the power of the state. This parade with Jesus is a movement of spirit that embraces the humble power of God coming to the world. It gives the nameless a name, and a little bit of hope for life to come.

Two parades. Which one would you have followed?

The one looking like the path to a good life will lead into a kind of death-in-life. The display of power has no hint of fairness. Those leading it don't care about justice or the common good. They don't care about the truth of God. As this parade continues, there will be loss of control, respect, honor, and love for life. Pilate washed his hands later that week, but they will always be bloody.

The other parade appears as if it is a losing path of weakness going toward a cross, toward death, but it is a path that actually gives life. Jesus lived, not for himself, but for others. It was in his love for God that others found a voice and a reason to love.

To love you. To love us. To love all. To love this world. Someone has said that what the world needs now is not survival of the fittest, but the survival of the wisest, and it is the wise one who knows that the world will not be recovered through the forces of violence, threat and war.

The cross of Jesus reminds us of the alternative - love, forgiveness, justice for all, compassion - the way toward life.

The week before us is holy.

I hope that we will walk into this week rededicated to the way of the cross, walking with Jesus, who leads us into the streets of our daily lives, calling us, challenging us and moving us to embrace the cross with all the little and big deaths in our own lives, and the life of the world.

I hope that, even as we remember the loss and sorrow of the cross this week, we will hold onto the simple wonder of a God who, in the midst of both our joys and sorrows, pleads for us to be united in care for the people in this world who live without any power and far too much injustice.

There were two parades that day in Jerusalem. There are still two parades happening in our world today. Which captures your attention? Which gets your support? Which do you follow?

I pray that you and I, and the Christian Church across this earth, will not comply with the systems that are seduced with the power of the world, seen in division, selfishness, war and violence.

I pray that we will always ask for forgiveness where we have complied with the ways of the world's power - and have wandered or been indecisive about the call to be followers of Jesus Christ - whose ways were known in the cross, bringing God's power of justice, hope, mercy and life for all.

Amen.

***

Seeking Transformation

December 13, 2015

Advent 3/C

Luke 1:39–56

This fall, as we've read The Story, we've covered over half of the Old Testament and learned about the Upper Story - that relentless pursuit of God to be in relationship with people.

This portion of Luke 1 is of the more beautiful accounts of the Upper Story where we watch God at work transforming a human life in a young woman named Mary.

In Advent, we wait and hope for transformation that is promised in Christ's coming again to this sorry and painful world. It's a promise to bring about a new creation.

The story of Mary and her acceptance of God's action through her is a glimpse of the transformation we await during Advent.

In those days Mary set out and went with haste to a Judean town in the hill country, where she entered the house of Zechariah and greeted Elizabeth. When Elizabeth heard Mary's greeting, the child leaped in her womb. And Elizabeth was filled with the Holy Spirit and exclaimed with a loud cry, "Blessed are you among women, and blessed is the fruit of your womb. And why has this happened to me, that the mother of my Lord comes to me? For as soon as I heard the sound of your greeting, the child in my womb leaped for joy. And blessed is she who believed that there would be a fulfillment of what was spoken to her by the Lord." And Mary said,

'My soul magnifies the Lord,
and my spirit rejoices in God my Savior,
for he has looked with favor on the lowliness of his servant.
Surely, from now on all generations will call me blessed;
for the Mighty One has done great things for me,
and holy is his name.
His mercy is for those who fear him
from generation to generation.
He has shown strength with his arm;
he has scattered the proud in the thoughts of their hearts.
He has brought down the powerful from their thrones,
and lifted up the lowly;
he has filled the hungry with good things,
and sent the rich away empty.
He has helped his servant Israel,
in remembrance of his mercy,
according to the promise he made to our ancestors,
to Abraham and to his descendants forever.'

And Mary remained with her for about three months and then returned to her home.

Dear Sisters and Brothers;

May you find life transformed by the news of a Savior who has come to this world and has promised to come again and make all things new.

It was a mild Saturday morning in December some 20 years ago. Like this year, no snow had yet covered the ground. I was coming out of my office when a guy about my age, entered. He was wearing a light jacket, white dress shirt and black dress slacks.

"Is there a pastor I could talk to?" he asked. I guess my blue jeans and sweatshirt didn't give me away. I replied "Well, I'm one of them. What can I do for you?"

"Do you have a couple of minutes?" he asked. I know from experience that whenever someone asks that question, that there's more than a couple of minutes of listening I'm going to be doing.

Taking off his jacket, he settled into my office and began to tell his story. In the first hour, I learned his name, Gino and how he had made his way to my office. That morning he had driven into town from the Twin Cities and abandoned his car in the Plaza Hotel lot. With no bag in hand and only a pack of cigarettes in his pocket, he started walking east down Clairemont and into Salem Baptist church across the road. They told him they couldn't help him, but said, "Go over to Trinity and see if the Lutherans might help."

As his comfort level with me grew, I learned that Gino was done waiting. He had waited long enough for the courage to open himself to a transformation of life. Now on this December Saturday morning – it was time. Gino was fleeing his way of life, and for his life. My office that Saturday morning had become the launching pad for the advent of a new future apart from life in the Mafia.

Gino hadn't planned the details when he decided it was time to flee the Twin Cities and the mob. The night before, he had been given an order to kill one his clients who had been repeatedly late in making loan payments.

As the second hour of listening began, Gino needed a cigarette break. He asked if I would go outside with him while he smoked. I proposed a walk so that I could steer free of the second-hand smoke. We headed outside and walked around the block. That was enough time for two cigarettes. A couple of people spotted me, honked and waved and then tossed a curious look toward Gino as they pulled away. Gino cowered each time a car would slow. His fear that someone from the mob had followed him and was about to act caught him between breaths.

As we settled back into my office, Gino told me that some months earlier he had been befriended by the waitress at the café he frequented each morning. Over time, they formed a friendship and the woman had invited him to her church. He started attending a bible study with her. For Gino, it was the glimpse into a way of life he had never known. To be with people outside the mob, to see that she didn't live under threat or dominance began to appeal to him. The Bible study opened his spirit. Gino began to see the Lower Story of his life being changed by the Upper Story of God.

To Gino's boss and other ranking members of the mob, his wayward tilt into mainstream life was concerning. Soon threats began to come down upon him. First they were gentle. "Quit seeing that woman and we'll forget that you started going soft." Later he was told, "You will stop going to that church and that bible study." As the threats intensified, Gino found that the transformation he was discovering was gaining a foothold deep inside him. The threats weren't enough for him to fall back into line with the mob.

If anything, they emboldened Gino to confess. He sought out the pastor of the church to see if he was a safe person in whom to confide. In that initial conversation, Gino hinted at his desire to bare his soul in hopes of finding forgiveness and a safe path to a new life. The pastor offered a second visit and Gino agreed. But what the pastor didn't tell Gino was that he was going to have a police officer waiting in the wings at that second visit.

Being astute to any potential threat, Gino's radar was dialed to high as he approached the church for that second appointment. Before he was ambushed by the pastor and police officer, Gino fled undetected. Hurt, confused and disappointed, Gino never went back to that church.

It pleased Gino's bosses in the mob to have him fall back into obedience, yet they were not ready to fully trust his allegiance. So, that order to kill one of his late-paying clients was going to put Gino to the test on the Saturday morning he sat in my office.

The day had started like any other in which he was ordered to kill. He arose early, dressed, cleaned his gun, grabbed a rug in which to wrap the body and a bag of lime to use at the point of burial. But on this morning, Gino was troubled. That Upper Story of a God who loves, forgives and promises a new life was colliding with the order he had been given.

As Gino was driving to pick up his accomplice to carry out this killing, the story of God was spinning through his brain. *Should I do what I've been ordered to do? I know I shouldn't do this. If I don't do this – I know they'll kill me. I know what I want. I know I want a new life. I know that church and my friend and that bible study had begun changing my mind, my heart, my soul.* The Lower Story of Gino's life was being transformed by a vision of the Upper Story of God.

Turning back toward his apartment to grab some clothes and valuables needed to start his new life, Gino realized the Mob was waiting nearby. Before he was detected, he fled. To Eau Claire. To the Plaza Hotel parking lot. To Trinity Lutheran Church. To my office.

By the end of the morning, Gino had told me of his hopes for a life, apart from the Mob. He did have a plan to travel to a distant part of the country where a friend would provide support. But he needed my help to get there. Providing him assurance that I would help him caused Gino to smile for the first time in the 2 ½ hours since he came in the door.

I took him to my home for lunch that day. He walked in the door and stopped. “What’s wrong, Gino?” I asked. He paused and slowly looked around the room and said, “I’ve never had a home like this. I’ve never known a life where there is peace and no one is threatening me. What’s it like?”

As we sat down for homemade soup and bread, we lit the candles in the Advent wreath on my table and we prayed together. Gino, my new friend and brother in Christ, had won my heart and I was watching a transformation take place before my eyes.

After lunch, we went to a teller machine so I could get cash to give him for a couple of tickets. He needed a bus to get to an Amtrak line leading away from Minneapolis in the pursuit of the new life he envisioned.

As we arrived at the Greyhound terminal downtown, Gino was speaking to me as if we had been friends since childhood. He was trying to figure out how he was going to contact me in the future to tell me about his new life. He also wanted to pay me back. But he didn't want to carry my name and phone number – and I agreed that was a good idea.

A few minutes later, a big black Cadillac pulled into the bus station lot. Gino's chest heaved. "Relax my friend, that's just the Limocab, that's the taxi service here in town" I assured him. Gino wanted to pray again and as he did he asked God to continue to the transformation that had begun in his life that morning. Then he hugged me. Left my car and walked into the bus station.

Every day for a year, I waited to hear from Gino. I prayed for him daily. Fighting back my own doubts that one can truly walk away from the mob and live, I prayed that Gino's transformation continued.

As heavy as my heart has been each time I've thought of Gino for the past twenty years, I believe that the transformation we all await – the new life safe and secure in the Upper Story of God is really about the glorious redemption of human life right now – your life, my life, Gino's life – thanks to a Savior who has come. However, we still wait, don't we?

My friends, may all the waiting you endure in your life – be lifted by the amazing love of a God who will also come again and make all things new.

Amen.

***

About the Author

Kurt Jacobson grew up in Rice Lake, Wisconsin. He holds a Bachelor of Art degree from Concordia College in Moorhead, Minnesota, with a double major in Business/Hospital Administration and Organizational Communications. He holds a Masters of Divinity degree from Luther Seminary in St. Paul, Minnesota. He served a year-long internship under Pastor Michael Button at Faith Lutheran Church, in Dickinson, Texas. Ordained into the Ministry of Word and Sacrament of the Evangelical Lutheran Church in America, Pastor Jacobson was called to serve Trinity Lutheran Church, in Eau Claire, Wisconsin, beginning in June 1988. In June 1999, he was installed as Lead Pastor. He retired from Trinity Lutheran Church in 2016.

Acknowledgments

This collection of sermons comes out of the worshiping community of Trinity Lutheran Church over the past twenty-eight years. My first thanks goes to the people of Trinity. I'm grateful they have listened to me and along the way found something of merit in my preaching.

My thanks to Pastor Mike Button who was my internship supervisor while serving Faith Lutheran Church, Dickinson, Texas. Mike taught me the practical methods of preaching and the art of developing sermons that bring the biblical text into the context of people's lives. His passion for preaching the Word and his constant encouragement has been among the best gifts given to me in ministry.

Thanks to Andra Palmer for having a vision to collect these sermons and for coordinating all the aspects of seeing this book through to publication.

I thank Steve and Anne Josephson for editing the final draft, and their encouraging and insightful comments.

In sum, I'm grateful to many people, from my parents who are models of faith, Sunday school teachers, college and seminary professors, pastoral mentors and colleagues who provided support, talked things over, read, wrote, offered comments, allowed me to quote their remarks and assisted the in the development of many of these sermons.

Finally, a specific thanks to Ryan Levesque and Dawn Fisher at eBookIt for their hard work and attention to the publishing and design process.

Bibliography

CPSIA information can be obtained
at www.ICGtesting.com
Printed in the USA
FSOW01n1637150416
19285FS